# The
# TESTIMONY
## I Never Wanted

## Overcoming Shame and
## Finding Purpose

### By
# Amy Helm Blackwell

Book Versions
Paperback ISBN: 978-0-578-60700-9
eBook ISBN: 978-0-578-60701-6
Copyright © 2019 Amy Helm Blackwell

# CONTENTS

Dedicated back to Jesus, the
One that gave me this story to tell.

# FOREWORD

I met Amy the way many of us meet for the first time these days. In her desperation and despair, she reached out to me through Social Media. She reminded me so much of myself in her pain that I felt an immediate connection. I shared with her the hope I discovered God offers us in our deep hurts, and the purpose that can truly be found in our pain.

Within the pages of *The Testimony I Never Wanted* you will follow along on Amy's amazing journey from pain to purpose. She will walk you through the steps of faith she took to be restored to her true self. You will marvel at how God is using every part of her past to bring help and hope to others - including you, dear reader.

Are you feeling like you're lost to past mistakes? That it's too late to live the life God has for you? Are you feeling desperate for a meaningful purpose? If you answered yes to any of these questions, then Amy 's story will bring hope to your heart.

Kim Crabill, Author,
*Burdens to Blessings:Discover the power of your story*
KimCrabill.org

# INTRODUCTION

As a child I heard many testimonies. Somehow, it always seemed that the person speaking in front of the church was reading from a movie script, their own Lifetime movie. I remember one day after leaving church I said to my daddy, "I don't have a testimony like theirs. How is the testimony of a little girl who prays in a barn for Jesus to come into her heart ever going to be something God can use?" I mean, my testimony was not filled with stories of parties, drinking, drugs, fights or finding Jesus in jail. I will never forget the words of my daddy, "Amy, you do not want to have that kind of testimony. Those are filled with pain and heartache that would have lasting consequences."

For years, I stressed myself out about walking that fine, "good Christian girl" line. It seemed easy, after all, I was homeschooled from third grade on. I lived on a dairy farm and fit nicely and comfortably inside my secluded, well-protected little bubble. I only listened to Christian music, watched "The Little House on the Prairie" series on TV and thought anything else would corrupt my little mind. At that age, I knew I did not want to be of the world; it looked so scary. I was often made fun of because of my firm stances on things, and yes, I was probably a bit legalistic. I knew I wanted to be like David, a man after God's own heart well, minus the adultery and murder of a man. I loved how he was called at such a young age, and I, too, wanted to take down my own Goliath.

I was a daddy's girl. If Daddy said it, I said it. If Daddy believed it, I believed it. If Daddy set things in stone, well I wore the stone around my neck as a necklace, beaming with pride. He was my compass, my "what do I do" in life. He was my go-to; whatever my daddy wanted, I wanted as well.

After Daddy's death, I felt alone, left floating out into the deep waters without a compass. My whole way of thinking was lost. I had never thought for myself, and when I did try I faced a lot of insecurities. I questioned everything I did or said.

Ultimately today, my testimony is one that Daddy said I would not want to have, but here it is. It is one that does not involve drugs, alcohol or wild living. I did not end up in a jail cell, but that does not mean Satan did not use what was on hand to tempt and confuse. The thought patterns that originated in my childhood erected my very own mental jail cell. In other words, I was a prisoner behind bars of a different kind, strongholds that began their construction at a very early age.

Let's go back to where it all started.

# CHAPTER 1

# Panic For Perfection

As a young girl, I was taught by my daddy that perfection and hard work equaled success and praise. It's not a surprise that I looked at my spiritual life in the same way.

I was very stressed at a young age, feeling the weight of the world on me. If I were asked to describe my childhood with one negative word, that word would be "panic," but still in my eyes my childhood was amazing. I can still remember the innocence of the little girl I was before I began kindergarten. Public school was the beginning of my insecurities; I lost bits and pieces of my self-worth and value with each passing year after that. I guess no one ever sat down and asked how I was doing or how I felt about things. I remember what it was like holding so much inside and not being able to get it out. Now that I have my own children, I realize the importance of sitting down and discussing their day with them.

Learning in school was quite difficult for me. Kindergarten and first grade were not so bad because of the sweet teachers who treated me like the other students. I still remember clearly what awaited me in second grade and how it taught me I was "not pretty enough" and "not smart enough." One boy severely bullied me. He made fun of my hair, my clothes and called me "Amy Helm Dog," which was always followed with a dog bark. At the age of seven, I experienced full-blown panic attacks while trying to pick out clothes before heading to school in the morning. The bullying continued, as well as the name calling, and the mean boys always stole my candy.

What hurt the most was being singled out by my teacher; maybe she did not realize what she was doing, but it stayed with me for years. I read great while sitting in my daddy's lap in the evening, but when I was at school in front of my teacher and my classmates I became so anxious I could hardly get the words out. I felt like I was going to mess up, and I waited for that to happen. My teacher created two reading groups: the rabbit group and the turtle group. I was the only girl in the turtle group with all the unruly boys. One day the aroma of popcorn filled our school room, and the teacher said, "Today we are having a popcorn party!" We were all excited until she said, "Those of you in the turtle reading group will not be a part." As I sit here on my front porch writing, I still feel the emotions from that moment to this day.

Those were just a couple of the favoritisms that happened during that time, but each was imprinted onto my seven-year-old mind, making me believe I was not "good enough."

I wanted my teacher, and others, to like me. I wanted to be looked at the same as the other little girls. They had their pretty clothes, pretty hair and pretty teeth where I was a crooked-toothed, freckled-faced tomboy. My self-esteem was as low as my grades.

I was scared to ask for help with papers that I didn't understand, so I ended up guessing at answers and making very bad grades. My teacher had moved my desk to the back of the classroom so that I could be alone; I felt very isolated. I was given a sheet to work on, and I did not understand the directions. I started crying because I was scared to ask for help. I did the best I could, but apparently I did it wrong because she returned my paper with a BIG RED zero on it. That was my last year in public school. My parents thought it best to home school me and my brother. As I grew older, my fear of people grew as well, fear of confrontation, fear of speaking up or asking questions. I believed my job was to please everyone and do what I was told the best I knew how. That became my identity.

I loved being at home all the time with my momma. We joined the East Texas Homeschool group; we went to skating nights, park days, and my brother even dissected a frog. My friendship with a girl named Christin resulted from our participation in that group. She and I were so alike! I did not feel like an odd duck around her because we were raised pretty much the same, although she was way more girly and more outgoing, not shy like I was. From ages eight to sixteen we were the best of friends. We had late night talks that always included Dr. Pepper, raw oatmeal cookie dough (yes, raw eggs and we both survived!) and long talks on the phone about boys. I was devastated when she and her family moved back to Central Texas almost four hours away. It always seemed that the people I loved left me in some way. I did go to visit her on occasion and cried when leaving as I headed back to a friendless life.

Early on, I became exceptionally good at the whole peacekeeping thing in my family. I saw the things that caused fighting between my parents and took on the job of extinguishing the flames before they turned into wildfires. I managed to put out a lot of those flames but failed on many occasions. I discovered if the house was spotless, no fighting. If we stayed home and off the roads, no fighting. If I chose work over play, no fighting. There were many situations I could not defuse. One time, I was standing in the living room, having been awakened by yelling and fighting. "Please stop!" I pleaded. My daddy was so angry with my mom. I remember seeing Momma crying, and my heart broke for her. I stood there frantically as he stormed into their bedroom, got all her clothes, brought them into the living room where she and I were still sitting, threw them on the chair and said she could get her stuff and leave. I spoke up crying and begging him, "Please Daddy, no! Please stop!" Tears poured from my eyes; my arms and legs were shaking uncontrollably.

In my little mind, my whole life was falling apart. There I sat on the couch at fourteen years old. Did he not see what this was doing to me? I knew that in those moments of rage he was not thinking, because if he were he would never have acted like that. I know now that deep down under all that anger was a hurt little boy. So there I was, a little girl taking note of all that set my daddy off, and I worked hard each day to prevent those things from happening. *Oh, so he does not want us gone from home much and for long periods of time, I'll make sure to get Momma home faster from the store and never ask to go anywhere. OK, he doesn't want her to spend money so I'll make sure to put items back when she's not looking.* One time I was caught and got into trouble for this.

We were at the store, and Momma had told me and my brother we could each get a piece of candy. Now, Momma had a lot of stuff in her shopping cart, so I was flipping out on the inside. I quickly told her, "No thank you; I do not want any candy (when I really did). My brother grabbed a pack of gum (you know the kind with the baseball player on it that looks like chewing tobacco) and placed it on the checkout counter. In my little mind, it was worth hundreds and I had to stop it, but how? When my mom and brother were not looking, I quickly grabbed the pack of gum and hid it away. I had just saved a possible fight between Momma and Daddy because of a pack of gum, or so I thought in my mind. I didn't know details of things, but I did know that gum cost money and Momma and Daddy fought over money. Later, down the road, my brother was looking for his gum and could not find it. I became nervous at that point when Momma started looking, too. "Amy, have you seen it" she asked. "Um, well, um, no." Then I couldn't take it anymore and blurted out, "I put it back!" My momma asked why I did this, and I told her I did not know, even though I did know. For all they knew, I was just being a bratty little sister.

Another responsibility I took on was keeping the house

spotless. Every day I hit the ground running, getting to work cleaning. I developed some mad cleaning skills! I felt I could breathe and be peaceful when I was finished, (To this day I vacuum almost daily to relieve anxiety). All of the thoughts inside of me created a great panic to make sure everything was perfect in everyone's lives, in our household and even others'. If I was at someone else's house I'd start cleaning. My friend, Christin became aggravated at me for organizing her closet. Most moms loved it when I came to visit. I had this constant thought of doing what I could to make life better, and I did it everywhere I went. Once, my mom and I were at a teacher supply store, and as my mom was shopping for school and church items I began to organize and straighten the store's shelves. This behavior became something I did everywhere I went.

There were periods that home life was good but then something as small as Momma cutting her hair too short would set Daddy off on a rampage. I can still remember how uncomfortable I was when Daddy treated Momma like a stranger when she came home with shorter hair; I saw the concern and worry on her face. Knowing that Daddy did not like short hair, I made sure to never cut my hair shorter.

I loved Momma and would defend her many times. As the years went on and I became a Daddy pleaser, I began to disrespect my momma. I saw how Daddy talked to her and his actions were not respectful at times, so I treated her with disrespect also. I heard him say negative things to her about what he felt she was not doing right.

Daddy was very hard on my older brother also. I saw this and thought I would be the smart one and work extra hard at being better at everything related to work and life. I wanted to please Daddy so much that when he praised me for something I did well, I soaked it up like a sponge. Daddy, in my eyes, was still a good man even though there were things inside of him he had brought from his own childhood. My momma told me stories of how my daddy never heard his own parents say they loved him growing up, and he was told not to come running to them when he failed at his business opportunities.

My internal dialogue was on continuous playback... *work, stay home, do not spend money, choose work over fun.* I told myself, "Be perfect, Amy." What I saw and heard was engraved on my young mind. I did not realize this until many years down the road, many wrong roads. I worked as hard as I could to be a perfect Christian and daughter, not knowing that I was creating a monster.

I wanted to please God; that was my heart's desire. I looked at others' choice and thought to myself, "I will NEVER do that or put myself in that situation." I mean, how could I? I was working way too hard to be perfect. I stayed home away from the world and lived in my little bubble, safe and secure. For almost twenty-eight years I lived my life in that bubble. My so-called work to perfection was based on my own works, the strength of my own flesh, almost as if I was saying *"God, I'll prove to you that I can be better than the others! I'm not like them."* I was not praying and growing spiritually even though I had convinced myself I was. I mean, I had not committed one of those catastrophic sins in my life, you know, one of the BIG ones! I had my purity card signed and on hand. I did not party or rebel; I stayed home and out of trouble. I saw other teens rebelling and thought, *"How could they hurt their parents?"* I could not fathom hurting my parents or bringing shame to their name.

I was the peacekeeper so naturally I would not bring in more chaos. We had enough of that behind closed doors. I was so worried about pleasing my earthly father and Heavenly Father and being good enough for them that I had completely missed knowing the glory of God, and HIS GRACE for me. I can picture Him looking at me, tapping His foot and thinking, *"Come on Amy, come to me."* I was too busy trying to be perfect in my own power and control of myself.

The verbal abuse continued until I was around sixteen years old, and I could drive then. During one fighting episode between my parents, I left and went to my brother's and stayed for a few days. I had seen and heard so much over the years and had the "flight mentality." Before then, I would just run and hide in my closet, crying and praying it would stop. On this particular day, it all came to a boil, and I just couldn't take it anymore. The harsh words, the yelling and belittling coming from my daddy to my momma sent me into a panic, so I ran. Let me tell you, it felt good. I felt like I was making a statement with my actions that I couldn't make with my voice. Later on in life, this became a coping skill that was not good BUT it was my only way to fight back. FLIGHT!

After a few days of being at my brother's house, I came back home and walked straight into my bedroom. Daddy followed me. I'll never forget his bright blue eyes filled with tears as he looked at me and said, "I'm so sorry for what I have put you through over these years; it'll never happen again." He asked for my forgiveness. "Of course, Daddy, I forgive you," I immediately said. Remember, I loved and respected my daddy and nothing had ever changed that. When I looked at him, all I saw was my hero, a man who lived each day NOT perfect but showing me ways to apply Christ in my life.

I chose to see the good, not the bad, and I chose forgiveness always. I chose not to ever speak about the abuse because it was not my identity, or was it? Rather, I pretended to keep that "Brady Bunch" image alive for me more than anything else. I even went so far as to say I never heard negative words from home. Deep down I really tried to believe that, and I thought I believed it since no problems came from it. Not yet anyway. For the next three years, from what I could see the fighting came to a stop. Daddy was even getting out more and doing things other than working all the time. Daddy was finally starting to enjoy life, and I loved seeing that.

My brother had married young, at nineteen years of age, and a couple of years later, for whatever his reasons, he pulled away from our family. This completely crushed our family. As a young girl, I had spent many hours daydreaming that he and I would grow old singing together, just like Donny and Marie. We had grown up close together but then had grown apart one month after the other. This was the same brother I literally had taken a beating for ten years earlier.

I was around seven years old, and my brother had just turned eleven. We had spent the night with our grandma, Opal, a few weeks earlier, and a flashlight had been broken in the spare bedroom where we had been sleeping. My brother was turning it on and off, over and over. The switch fell off and he hid the parts on the shelf in the headboard. Daddy asked us if we had broken it; I quickly said, "No I did not," knowing that my brother had. My brother insisted he had not broken it either. I stood there, silent, but did not tell on him. Daddy dismissed my brother and asked me again. Over and over I said, "No sir." Daddy did not believe me because I had been caught in a few lies prior to this, so he laid me over his knee and whipped me. He stopped and said, "You going to tell the truth now?" "But Daddy, I promise I never did it," I pleaded. Not believing me, he continued to whip me. I could barely catch my breath from crying. I had spankings before, but nothing this painful and drawn out. Of course, those other spankings were very much deserved; this one I did not deserve. Finally, I said, "Yes, I did it." It was a lie but I just wanted him to stop.

I went into the bathroom, turned around to look into the mirror that hung on the back of the door. I was covered in red marks from my lower thighs to my bottom. I hurt so badly my skin was pulsating from so much pain. Momma came in to be with me and saw how bad it was. I whispered, "Where is Daddy?" She said he was sitting on the porch crying. I found that to be confusing. She said he felt bad he had to whip me. My legs were trembling so badly I could barely walk. When I went to bed it was painful to lie down.

I curled up in my Cabbage Patch sheets and tried not to think of what had just happened. I was already scared of my daddy but this pushed it over the edge, knowing even if I had not done anything wrong I still was in trouble. I lay there and cried myself to sleep. I was so confused and did not know how to cognitively process what had happened at that tender age of seven. The next morning the bruises were so bad I was not allowed to go to school, and I did not go again until they had faded some.

Ten years later on a camping trip with my family, that story somehow came up. My brother laughed and said, "Yeah, I did it and was in the hallway hearing the beatin' Amy was getting. I felt bad, but Daddy had already started whipping her, so I was too scared to come forward with the truth." Everyone was quiet….my daddy was sitting there in a lawn chair. As I saw the blood drain from his face, I saw grief as he rose up and said in a painful, stern voice, "Do you know what happened to her? I whipped her over and over until she told the truth!" I piped up and said, "See Daddy, I was not lying but then had to lie to stop you." Daddy looked at me and said he was so sorry. I just said, "It is alright." I was happy he finally knew the truth after all those years. It was not too long after that trip that my brother started to drift slowly away from the family.

I was so thankful at that time I had my cousin who had become my best friend and "partner in crime." We did everything together; he was there at every major event in my life from wedding dress shopping, to studying for my real estate exams, and he was there waiting in the car as I came running out with excitement after I'd passed my test. I bet we still hold the record for the number of movies we've seen together. He and I were like peas and carrots, peanut butter and jelly – a true friendship. We were so close, and I knew I could always count on him to be there for me. His being there sure helped me to cope with the void of missing my brother. My cousin later had some personal family dealings that left him hurt and upset. He turned to another road that I was not on, which completely devastated me. Looking back, I wish that I had been a better friend to him, gone to him and encouraged him to stay around me and my family no matter what, but I did not. It was years before I saw him again. That was a deep, hidden loss for me, but I just added that to the list of other losses in my life.

Because my brother had drifted away from our family, Momma fought depression and developed ulcers from worrying; Christmas that year was not the same. Momma had no desire to shop or to decorate for the season, which was unlike her. That year, I did all the shopping and even bought and wrapped my own gifts. In years past, she and I were the Black Friday shoppers and early Christmas decorators for the season. You could literally see our house from a mile away because of all the Christmas lights! I did not understand why this had happened to all of us, and I was determined never to break my parents' hearts as I had seen happening. My greatest fear, even today, is that one of my children will reject me when they get older.

Growing up, my passion was to be as successful in business as my daddy had been. He had poured all the ingredients for success into me, and because of that I had my own real estate business at the age of fifteen with my mom. We flipped houses before flipping houses was a big thing. I moved on up from my little store located in our enclosed back porch; A-Mart was the name. I had candy and goodies to sell, and sell I did! It was there that I learned to count money and how to make a profit.

As I became older, I found myself pulled toward the idea that I needed a boyfriend, but deep inside I did not really want one. Now, that does not make sense, but that was my focus to find a guy young like my momma had, to get married and milk cows. No one ever told me otherwise. I really needed someone to tell me that it was all right not to have a boyfriend and it was okay not to marry young. That was the path my parents took, and I was on the path to do it their way. I was bound and determined to do things the way they did them. I had never done much thinking on my own, and if I did I felt badly, thinking I was forsaking my daddy's wisdom.

At nineteen years old, I'd just come out of a three-month relationship where I really thought this guy was "the one," but I found myself brokenhearted once again. This guy had all the characteristics I had been praying for. He vowed to be pure until marriage, was a godly young man who was in college nearby, but God led him another way. I was hard on myself after that breakup thinking, *Am I not good enough for him? Did his parents not like me? Was it because of my lack of education?* I had always been embarrassed about being homeschooled; a lot of people turned up their noses at that. What better thing for me to do in my frustration than to tell God, "I will not bother with a guy and will focus on You." That was my plan.

Apparently I did not mean that because a few weeks later I was venting about my relationship woes to a lady who was helping with Wednesday night kids' church. She chimed in and said to me that I should meet her son. I had known this family all my life, but her son was six years older than me and I did not know him well. As she mentioned him to me, I had a flashback in time. It was an Easter Sunday sunrise service years earlier. I was thirteen or fourteen, I believe, and I had seen him there and thought he was a cute OLDER college guy. Later, on the way home, I was looking out the car window at the trees going by, and out of nowhere the thought ran through my mind, *"You'll marry him."* Wait, what? This was a very weird thing to think, and that was the last time I remembered that thought until she mentioned him to me.

Hearing this from the guy's mom, my mind was boggled, *"Could this be God's plan? What about this whole promise to focus on God and not guys?"* We were later officially introduced after church one Sunday morning. Later that day, he came over and we talked out by the working cattle pens; he asked about my brother, and I thought "Here goes." I explained in a few words that at the moment my brother had chosen not to be around us. It was embarrassing to tell this guy while wondering what he must think of me and my family, that my own brother didn't want to be around us. My family was broken, and I didn't know what to do with the brokenness or how to explain it. It was never supposed to be like this.

The next week, he and I went out to the fanciest place in town (The Golden Corral!), and I gave him the whole spiel about "I do not drink, party and I'm saving myself until marriage. If you have a problem with that you can just leave now." He looked puzzled; apparently he had never been told that by a girl. That speech had driven many boys away before, and I was waiting for it to be the same this time. However, it was nice to hear him say he respected that of me.

We did not see each other very often because he lived over one hour away; most of our time was spent talking on the phone. A few months later he proposed. Daddy had given him his approval, so that, along with that long-ago thought, made me believe that this was all God's plan. I just thought it was what I was supposed to do. My mind was wired to please others and to make their lives good, so that is what I did. This guy loved Jesus, Check! He had a good, godly upbringing, Check! He wanted a family farm of his own, Check!

We married in October of that very same year, and I was praying my brother, who was still away from the family, would come to our wedding. Before the wedding started, the photographer was taking my pictures in the sanctuary; in walked my brother with my niece and nephew! I completely lost it. I ran to him, trying not to trip over my big, poofy wedding dress. The photographer captured that moment when we hugged, my face covered in tears. "You came!" I was happy because now all my family was there for my special day.

The honeymoon, well it was not as I thought it would be. I had waited until marriage to give myself to my husband just as I was supposed to do. The pain was so bad I found myself sitting in a bath of hot water, crying, just wanting to go home. I was so upset and scared that I called from Mexico back to home to my friend, Stacey. She had given me "the talk" before we were married; I knew nothing much of sex. I tried to make the best of our trip, even if I was in discomfort, because it was my first time to see the beautiful ocean. I was hard on myself because I felt broken, and I was letting my husband down. I felt I was disappointing as a wife already.

After we got back home, I found out from my gynecologist that the pain I had would continue until I either had surgery to repair the issue or have a baby. "Um, no thank you," I quickly told my doctor. I certainly was not having any kind of surgery, and I was not planning on having a baby for a few years. My husband was very understanding and patient about it, but the trauma and pain from it all left me wanting nothing to do with it. I even thought, *"God, I was a good girl, and this is what I get for it?"* We had talked about getting pregnant a couple of years after marriage, but I think the earlier trauma and the late night baby duty created a mental and emotional block. It was a struggle for me and left me feeling like I had again failed.

After the wedding, I moved to where my husband lived and worked, which was one and a half hours away from my parents. I was not ready for that shock. Being away from my parents was extremely difficult for me, and I was not really prepared for it at all. In a lot of ways, I was still very much a child. I went home every weekend to visit and wash clothes. Our small house did not have a place for a washer and dryer, and I was too scared to go to the laundromat. My husband worked late on some nights, and I would call my momma crying. I was not used to being alone.

I still clung to every word my daddy said and reminded myself of who I was, which was who my daddy was. Even then, as a married young woman, if Daddy made suggestions, I did it. If he made suggestions of where to sell real estate or where to buy the right home, I did what he suggested.

It wasn't that he was controlling. I just had the mindset to listen to only him. I was not comfortable making any decision without Daddy's thoughts on it; I wouldn't allow myself to trust anyone else's opinions, including my own.

I'm thankful that we did not have a washer and dryer and that I went home all those weekends. One year later, on November 14, 2001, I received a call that placed my emotions on lockdown. I was off work that day and thought I'd put the Christmas tree up early. As I plugged the Christmas tree lights in, the phone rang. My daddy had a heart attack and died; there was nothing I could do to change that. He was only forty-eight years old. I was not mad at God, was I? I knew Daddy was in a better place without pain. Yes, he was a broken man, but he surely ran a pretty good race and served God well in my book. Even in his brokenness, Daddy had a heart for Kingdom building. My daddy was my guide and my compass, so what was I supposed to do now?

When he died, I had a feeling of emptiness. I felt like a train that had been going full speed down the track, and all of a sudden the engine blew and came to a standstill. I felt such deep loss, but it was easier to brush it off and say, "He's with Jesus." I'd felt loss before, but THIS LOSS was a new kind for me. I remember leaving the hospital, and I was in the back seat looking out the window up at the stars. "Can he see me," I thought. Did God allow him to see me one last time before leaving? My identity had been wrapped up in my daddy all my life, so how was I going to face tomorrow? I even had the thought after he died that it would not be the same having my own children, now that he was not here to see them.

It was hard watching Momma try to find her new place in life. She had been with my daddy since she was fourteen years old and was lost as to what to do when he died. I watched everything my parents had worked so hard for slowly vanish, and my mom was naïve as to what was going on. It was hard on me also. I wondered, *"Who am I and what do I do?"* I had always been Steve Helms' daughter, and now he was not here. Like all the other times, though, I brushed the emotions away and worked at making my life as perfect as possible. I knew what "not perfect" looked like and wanted no part of that. It was looking like I had lost control of my life. *Why, God, why! First my brother left us, then my mom's heartache from that, the loss of my friends, and now You take Daddy from me!"* The dream and desire for that perfect family unit had been broken in so many more places, and it was heartbreaking to see the crumbled pieces that were left behind.

It was hard to accept love from those around me after that. I pushed away the people with whom I had once been close. The hurt hidden within showed up with me putting up thick walls that were guarded by my cold, harsh appearance. For twenty-eight years all appeared to be "cookie cutter" perfect in my little bubble that sat right in the center of my fairytale land; I had convinced myself that it was. I had made my bubble very comfortable, and mess, well it was not allowed!

All my hard work was paying off, it seemed. If something made me the least bit stressed, I shut it down and out of my life. Less stuff and less people equaled less stress. I suffered from crippling anxiety that I hid very well. In fact, I didn't even know it was anxiety at the time, as it did not have a name in my head. Nonetheless, I was very aware that something was going on inside of me. Even if I had no clue why, I was having panic attacks over the weirdest of things. My chest was tight, and I felt that each word or thought made it tighter.

In the kitchen when cooking, I became anxious, and I became "panicky" when cleaning the house. I was always cleaning, and the house had to be spotless so that I would not become more anxious. I then would look at the house and would experience a sense of calmness as it looked perfect. I did not like being away from the house, and when I was, my heart raced as I tried to do all that I could to get back home. As soon as I returned home, I felt an immediate sense of relief. I could not put my finger on why I felt this way; I just knew I wanted to be normal. But what was normal? What was I shooting for as a target? I was a train wreck waiting to happen.

I thought that I had this life figured out. Devoted wife and mom, Check. Being a good steward with what God had given me, Check. It had been "easy as pie keeping my nose clean" as my daddy would say. I stayed at home, and really I had no one with whom I was close. It did seem that when I tried to get close to someone they would move away. I had friends, but I would not dare tell them of the battles I had inside. I could not – *what would they think of me?* I had no accountability (why would I need that?). But panic? I lived with panic all the time. I stressed if I spent money. I had a panic attack if I was in a store because I had this urgency to get home. I would wake up, go to work cleaning the house and never sit down. I felt badly if I did anything fun or for myself. If my newly born son had a "Nana's night" I felt like I was being a bad mom. I was taught that "you have kids, you stay at home with your kids." I always had this dialogue running through my head, "Is this what I'm supposed to do?" I always thought I was going to do the wrong thing and was NEVER sure of myself. It was mentally exhausting.

I simply assumed that this was me and how I was naturally wired. I did not put all this together with my childhood. I had no hard feelings for anyone, so why would I need to have healing, right? I wore my masks very well; I had one in every color. I was walking a fine line, and that is what the enemy wanted me to think. Satan had been taking notes on me for years. He had seen the wounds, the secret pains and voids. He also saw that I was blocking it all out. I had not received the much-needed healing from all those things. I was blinded and very naïve. Satan was waiting for the perfect moment to attack. Honestly, I was such an easy target; I was like a sitting duck or a deer caught in the headlights. He knew I was only as strong as my human flesh would allow. Remember, that's what I was going for: SUPER AMY! I had created a monster.

By May 2004, my mom had sold the dairy farm where I grew up. She gave me half my inheritance to put down on a poultry farm. My husband and I, along with our one-year-old son, had moved to a very small town where the poultry farm was located. What a blessing that I could give my kids the farm life I had growing up, I felt. What was even greater was that three years prior, my daddy had gone with us to see this farm before he died; I felt he was a part of the farm in some way. Before my marriage, my daddy and I had been searching for a farm; the dairy industry had left our area so that dream was no more. Hence, the poultry business was the next best thing to do.

In the fall of 2006, we welcomed our blue-eyed, blonde-haired baby girl, and she was so beautiful. When she was born, the doctor held her up for me to see, and UP went her little leg like a slingshot, all the way to her head. The back of her leg looked like her knee. It was a scary moment, thinking that something was wrong; however, x-rays showed that everything would go back to the right place after a few days. It had been an easy delivery, and I was ready to go home.

I was so blessed! I knew that God had big plans for my children. When I was a teenager, I prayed what seemed like a very weird and outrageous prayer. I prayed for God to make me barren if He knew my children would rebel against Him. Because of that, I knew my children were going to be used for Him in some way.

The next couple of years flew by. During that time, my momma had met another man, and I just could not accept him. It caused our relationship to be very awkward. Part of me was so dead inside; the loss of my daddy, not being close to my brother, and now the relationship with my mom was torn because of some guy. The loss within from the torn-apart family was terrible. It was not supposed to be this way. As things in my life began looking more and more unlike a cookie cutter, it caused even more panic inside of me. I had no one to talk to about this. I needed my daddy. If he was here, everything would be all right because I would be safe and at peace in his thoughts.

# CHAPTER 2

# Pop Goes The Bubble

April 2008 - It was a beautiful, sunny day. I remember this day like it was yesterday. I had been married to my husband for almost eight years; he and I, along with our kids, were out checking cows. I even remember the very place where we were in the pasture and thought about how blessed we were to be able to give our kids the same life we both had growing up. I was very content in my perfect little bubble life.

One night the phone rang, and it was a girl who apparently had the wrong number A few minutes later she called again; I again said, "You have the wrong number." As I was hanging up the phone, I heard her say in a broken voice, "Please I do not know what to do. I need help. My life is falling apart." I froze as fear flooded my body. I said nothing because I did not know what to say. I did not know how to relate to her. I did not do messy. A few seconds passed as I sat there and breathed into her ear; CLICK, she hung up. This conversation on this day would later be a reminder many years later.

Middle May 2008. I walked into the house after videoing my husband and our kids jumping on the trampoline. My daughter was running around in circles with static in her hair, yelling that her daddy was a horsey and he was bucking her off. This video had the last captured moments of us all together before my life as I knew it would end.

The phone rang, and it was my mom. She asked if I had a MySpace account, and if so could I check to see if my niece was on there (I did not have MySpace and only used the "free internet" for my Ancestry.com addiction.) I went online to figure MySpace out and thought, *"Cool. I'll see who I can find."* I typed in a few old friends' names, and then my curious mind thought of an old boyfriend (the one my daddy did not think much of and prayed I would let go). He was one of those guys who did not have any goals for his future, and that was a BIG no-no in my family. I was sixteen when I met him through my best friend, Christin; I'm not sure why we were together for over two years. I really regretted our relationship because I missed out on a lot. He had a temper and even shattered the windshield of his truck when we were in an argument driving down the road. I wanted to remove myself from him and broke up with him every few months, it seemed. I always felt like I had to stay with him. Why was that? He was nothing like the man I prayed for, and yet I felt trapped by his presence. I gave away my life, even when I felt my strongest. WHY?

Here I sat, sending a message to my ex-boyfriend

telling him all about my life. I was really bragging because I had checked off everything on my list; I had done it! I had my marriage, my children and my farm. He was still in the same place after all these years. Wow, I thought, *"Thank you God that I did not end up staying with him."* In my prayers that night I even thanked God that my husband was a good and hard-working man. Even though my marriage had been like most, having its struggles at times, I was a faithful, devoted wife. I was very protective of our home, but I was so naïve that I could not see the door that I had just opened. It was a door that had been opened into almost two years of my youth, filled with my innocent life with my daddy. It was as if I was sitting down with this guy and reading a book about my past. Happiness flooded those empty places. I heard the words of my daddy flowing from his mouth as well as mine. It had been almost ten years since we had talked, since we had broken up for the fifth and the final time. I thought it was just going to be a one time, catching up kind of message, like he was that guy I was thankful I did NOT marry, remember? So why worry about my heart?

**Keep your heart with all diligence;**
**for out of it springs the issues of life.**
**Proverbs 4:23**

I did not know that the tucked-away, painful voids that I had been ignoring and pretending were not a big deal were going to be filled and filled with beautifully disguised and decorated sin. The talks about my daddy made me feel more excited about having our next conversation. Remember when this or that happened? It made me happy; my daddy made me happy. My daddy had been dead now for seven years by this time, but just like that I was hooked.

At first, I did not know I was hooked but I did know it was wrong because I did not tell my husband. Again, I thought my conversations with my ex-boyfriend were innocent and that I had everything under control. I found myself wanting to talk to him more about my family and things of the past. Honestly, talking to him made me feel sixteen again, all fun things that I thought were innocent. In my mind I was still thinking *"I am thankful I did not marry this guy…"* Seriously, like I had a dream years before that I had married this guy; I woke up in full panic and quickly looked over at my husband sleeping. I was so relieved the dream was just that, a dream, and not real. I kept talking to him, even knowing how I felt about him. I thought I had everything under control, but this was my first encounter with deception. Two weeks passed, and I was a wreck emotionally. I had never felt all these emotions and was trying to juggle what had become a very sinful life. I was not myself, as you can imagine. I was losing weight, not eating from the worry and fear because of what I was doing. My husband asked what was wrong because I was spaced out.

What was this! The THIS was taking over like a cancer spreading uncontrollably; I had never dealt with anything like this. It felt as if I was covered with a heavy blanket that was suffocating the life out of me, and I did not know what to do. I questioned myself, *"How can I be married and want a friendship with this guy?"* By this time, he told me he had never stopped loving me, blah, blah, blah, and all that pretty talk. I felt more entangled in this growing mess day by day.

Three week later, I found myself asking for a divorce and thought, *"There is no way my family will just let me leave."*

Maybe deep down that's what I was hoping would happen to save me from the choices I had made; at that time I could not pull away from the addiction. Soon after, my husband and I were at the divorce lawyer's office agreeing to the terms of our divorce. It's hard to explain, but part of me wanted to fight for my marriage, while the other part was hooked to the other guy. In my twisted, confused mind, I threw my family away. Oh gosh! What was wrong with me! To justify my actions, I of course looked at everything that was wrong in our marriage for reasons for divorce. For the next sixty days, I felt so many different emotions, ones that left me numb, mad, sad, bitter and happy, but that didn't last. They were similar to the emotions of an addict where the high only lasts for a moment, then other emotions come in. I had never been through this kind of back and forth emotional roller coaster in my life.

By then, my husband knew about my emotional affair, and so did our small town. I began walking a road of shame; I felt dirty and worthless. The talk in town just drove me further away. I saw someone in the store who had been a friend (I mean, was supposed to have been a friend. She had even come to see me in the hospital when I had my daughter); she completely ignored me. I felt even dirtier and even more rejected. This pushed me more deeply into isolation. *"This is what this feels like? This is the end of respect from others as well. I can't believe this is what has become of my life. It was a life that I worked so hard in perfecting, so how did it come to THIS?"*

My husband and I continued to live in the same house. I was still cooking, cleaning and washing clothes for him; of course, I did, I cared and loved him still. Deep down in the foundation of my heart, underneath all that sin suffocating my life, I did not want the divorce, but I could not break the hook that dug deeply into the very depths of my flesh. The once highly involved churchgoer I had been now dropped off the face of the earth; no one ever came, sat down and spoke to me, or us as a couple.

It was the final day the divorce papers were signed by the judge. Because of a feeling of care and some guilt, I left most of my inherited money and assets in the farm. Even in my confused state of mind, it was still very important for me to leave the farm intact for our kids. I have never been attracted to money, so it was easy leaving it all there; the farm was for our children's future. I went back to our house to move out. I was so numb as I walked through the house, looking around, replaying my life there and the kaleidoscope of memories. My ex-husband was not there at first, and I called my mom crying and saying I could not do this. She told me it would be all right, but that was not what I needed to hear. I needed someone in that moment to speak to my heart. I needed help! *Someone please shake me back to face reality so I can fix this!*

My ex-husband walked in and was going to help me move some things out. I was moving, yet my mind was in slow motion as I tried to figure out what had just happened. I wish I had been strong, stood up and said, "I'm going to do what I have to do to save my family," but I didn't know how to go in that direction at all. I told my ex-husband, "I don't want to lose my family." I was thinking, "*Has nothing of who I was for the first twenty-eight years of my life mattered? Was one*

*mistake worthy of all the other good in me to be washed away?"*
I stood up from the floor as I felt the life drain from the
bottom of my feet. This is it. This really is happening; how
did this happen? I could hardly pick up my feet as I walked
down the hallway to leave my once-home. Panic from failure
and all the shame weighed heavily on my chest.

I drove away in my car out into a world from which I
had worked so hard to protect myself, a world about which I
had not one clue. But here I was out in it, feeling worthless,
guilty and full of shame. It was not going to be a pretty
transition. I walked into what felt like the den of lions
without one ounce of strength or dignity. And God, well
why would He love me? I had failed Him and my family so
the game was over for me, I felt. I had blown my one chance
to get it right. I told myself repeatedly that I would NEVER
deserve forgiveness. I had done something I thought I would
never do; I had hurt my husband and our children. Although
my self-talk was not heard or seen by the outside world, it
became a very destructive thing to me on the inside.

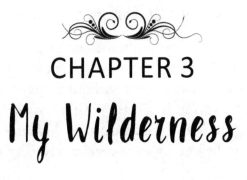

# CHAPTER 3
# My Wilderness

Days, weeks and months went by. Drowning, but not dying, is what I felt like every day. The guy that I had thrown away my life for, well, he was no more. I grew to hate him, and seeing him reminded me each day that he was a part of destroying my world, the world he knew I loved because I told him that in the beginning.

I put on the "mom mask" when I had my kids, as they were my oxygen and they were the only good thing I had left in my life. When they were not with me, all I did was cry and wait for them to come back. I was deeply mourning the loss of my family, and I wanted the pain to go away. I did not want to feel or think about the depth of my loss. I found myself digging my fingernails deeply into my wrists and arms, just so that for a moment I wouldn't think but only feel the physical pain. I remember seeing things like a billboard at a church giving the statistics for children with divorced parents. Alcohol, drugs, promiscuity, suicide and depression were among other things listed, only adding to the thought of *"Because of me, my children are forever wounded."*

One night I was so immersed in pain. I remember crying outside in my driveway. I desperately missed my family. I cried and screamed without a sound coming out of my mouth, sitting in a fetal position, rocking back and forth, feeling the gravel underneath me. My arms ached from remembering the lost nights of rocking my daughter to sleep.

I went to church with my mom and cried through each song and each sermon. I read in the Old Testament about judgment, never reading the grace-filled words of Jesus in the New Testament. I felt that I did not deserve the New; I deserved the Old. I deserved judgment. Saying that I felt ashamed was an understatement; there must have been another word I could use to describe how I felt.

I would pretend at times that I was still married. Once I remember going to have my hair cut. The lady asked things about me; was I married, did I have children, you know, all the small talk. I could not tell her I was divorced, not me! I just could not say it! I never thought I would ever have to say those words from my once perfect little mouth, but here I was answering her with a big, fat lie. *"Yes, I'm married."* I proceeded to tell her all about my life as it used to be.

December 2008.

Momma said she saw an old friend of mine at the school while she was picking up my niece and nephew. He and I had not seen each other in years. Later on that week I was making a list to send out Christmas cards (which I mailed out as if I was still married to my first husband hoping most would not know I was divorced). Merry Christmas from us; yes, I had a very warped sense of thinking. As I was making the list, I thought to myself, *I will call this old friend and get his address so that I can mail one to him.* I called and we talked for a few minutes, just long enough to get his address and ask about his family. I didn't think any more about him until a few days later I received a call from an unknown caller; it was him. There he was with that voice I had always recognized. I found myself really enjoying our catching-up time.

Let me take you on a stroll way back to when he and I first met. I met this friend fifteen years earlier at around age twelve through our homeschool group. He was my first boyfriend at age fourteen, my first kiss (if you can even call it a kiss). That was the age Momma had met Daddy, so I thought my relationship with him would happen the way theirs had started out. He was helping me feed baby calves and stole a kiss by the milk tank. Nothing says romance like the smell of fresh cow milk and manure! He came over and helped me with my dairy chores, and I thought I was hot stuff when he invited me to a Dallas Holm concert with his church.

I remember making all those long distance phone calls that cost ten cents per minute. Daddy only allowed me a short time to talk; he would always ask when he heard me on the phone, "Whose dime is that? Better be that boy's!" Looking back, I was so innocent, being naïve to heartbreak and rejection. It was so devastating when he broke up with me. That was a new feeling and I felt myself questioning who I was, looking into the mirror and picking myself apart. I was still very much a tomboy and did not have a clue about being girly. Nevertheless, he and I remained friends throughout our teen years. Like clockwork every couple of years he would ask me to be his girlfriend again, and I would jump at the opportunity. Like normal, it would last a couple of weeks, and I would graciously let him go at his request. I saw him on many occasions, and he even worked for my dad some in the summers. That's how our story began.

Here we were, all those years later catching up on old times. I was eating up the stories that he told about the once respectable me. He even went so far as to say he had always thought that I was anointed by God and that he had spent all those years telling people he should have married Amy Helm. I soaked all that up because of all the past rejections from him, and I did not feel like the Amy he was speaking about anymore. When he said those things to me, I felt so ashamed of myself and what I had done. I made choices that this Amy he was speaking of said she would never make, although somewhere deep inside it was nice hearing about what I used to be like. He was a guy that had called me for spiritual advice in our teen years. I was the "good girl," and well, he had the "bad boy" image. His lifestyle did not fit inside of my pretty little bubble life. We started the same way I left my first marriage. To me, it did not matter if his divorce papers were filed long ago, it was still adultery.

I remember our first conversation because it's a reminder to me of how I kept choosing my selfish desires. On the phone, he found out I was divorced (which shocked him that Amy Helm would ever divorce). He said his marriage had its struggles, that he had filed for divorce long ago, but they were working things out. My next words were this, and I remember the exact place I was driving when I said them to him because it was that important. "Please think about not going through with a divorce; it's the worst thing I have ever done." In that moment, I allowed my pain to speak. The old Amy was speaking out, but then as the conversations continued, I found myself hooked again to the pretty things that were pouring into my ear, quenching a very dry and desolate self-image.

As I write this now, I think of what I could have done to possibly save their broken marriage, but instead my selfishness helped to finalize another split home.

**"Sin will take you farther than you want to go, keep you longer than you want to stay and cost you more than you want to pay." - Ravi Zacharias**

I was repeating a cycle that I had become hung up in. Worthlessness and shame created in me someone I said I would never be. After weeks of talking and me traveling to his worksite, our feelings for each other came out into the light. We had talked about getting married later that year, but with all the chaos going on around us, he called one day while I was at his sister's house and said, "Why don't we just get married when I come in from work?" With a look of shock on my face, I stared at his sister, mouthing the words, "He wants to get married now." With excitement and nervousness, I responded with a yes. There were parts of me that were happy; I mean, he wanted to be with me! The other parts of me knew this just was not a good idea with all the mess in our lives. He said that he thought by getting married it would fix some of the surrounding issues we were having.

On Friday, February 13, 2009 (I know, I know) we had a small and quick wedding outside with just close family. I could tell he was nervous. I did feel badly for him because I knew all too well the pain of a split home and knew he was having a hard time. He had just come out of a marriage and was still dealing with his own emotions. I was thinking to myself, *"I wish we could have started off different."* Deep down inside I knew our marriage was not blessed by God, that it would not have His favor, but I wished that it could have been. The wedding was short and sweet. Our marriage started off with drama all around, mostly self-induced by our sin. This was my so-called do-over marriage, and everything in me wanted to create a family again. There was a dead place in my life from the loss of my first marriage. I grabbed onto him in hope of bringing back to life all in me that was dead. There was a part of me that thought he had chosen me finally, but that was a twisted thought of which I became ashamed.

He ended our marriage after just two short weeks because of his own personal struggles, and once again my heart was broken by him. I wanted to save our so-called marriage, even though it was such a disaster; I did not want another failed marriage. On his birthday, I sat in the hallway of the courthouse, and he sat nearby; no words were uttered between us. It was killing me inside, and I wanted so badly to go over and say, "Please let's not lose our friendship," but I remained silent. I was sad for many reasons that day, one of them was I had not helped him as the longtime friend I had always been by encouraging him to save his first marriage. I am deeply sorry for the hurt and pain I caused everyone in that. I knew from that moment on that we would no longer have a friendship; gone was the friendship that had made it through all those little breakups when we were younger. We had always found a way to remain friends, but this time I knew it was over.

I had become very close to his sister, and she had been a good friend to me. She was trying as much as possible to help me navigate through this. As I was sitting on my front porch one evening reading my Bible, I was searching in hope that God would speak to me. I sent a text to her asking her to please pray for God to give me something, anything. There, sitting on the porch on my daughter's scooter, I opened my Bible, and with my eyes closed my finger landed in the middle of Isaiah 28:21

**That He may do His work, His awesome work; and bring to pass His act, His unusual act.**
**Isaiah 28:21**

I highlighted that verse and wrote March 2009 in the margin. Some days I believed God had a plan, but the other days I took my life into my own hands, as if trying to find a way to fix this all by magical potion, magical pill, anything. I could not believe God could take all this mess and sin and make anything great from it. I had set the bar too high years ago, and I had missed the mark. I felt that all of this was on me and that I had lost my chances at anything that would give me peace-purpose or any kind of self-worth.

My second marriage was over, and with that came many more regrets. My selfishness hurt so many innocent people because of my relationship and marriage to him. I hurt my second husband's loved ones with actions I chose not to stop. His children lost their dad, and now had a broken family because of me. I've always been told it takes two, which is true, BUT I did not have to be the other in the "party of two." I had fed myself to this world, and it was not pretty. My sin and my bad choices had produced things I had never been around, things that would attack me for months. From that relationship came some very eye-opening situations. I wanted my "bubble life" back so badly; if only I had that talked-about "redo button."

LESSON: Choose unrighteous ways, get unrighteous surroundings.

Walking a road not believing God was a hopeless and lonely place to be traveling, especially alone. Yes, I believed in Him and He was my Savior, but I did not believe Him. I felt that He could only make things new for others but not for me. I read scripture or heard things and told myself, *"It is just not true for me."* I was different. I loved the story of David, BUT again I felt it was different for me. Why had I convinced myself that I was different from all the rest? Maybe my perfection goals clouded my thinking.

I traveled further down this same road again, guy after guy, and found myself getting married for the third time to someone else from my childhood…always with someone from my past. See the pattern? It all started with online dating; who me? Never! I wish that it was true. I was encouraged by someone to join a dating site with the idea that I would meet someone outside of my area and that person would not have any knowledge I had money. I submitted my information and the desired distance. I should have used a wider range of distance, like the Middle East. Then who knows what would have happened.

A picture popped up with a familiar face. This person was a neighbor growing up; his family's farm adjoined our family's farm. We exchanged phone numbers and began texting. I was never interested in him in any way other than just friendship and conversation. As we caught up on each other's lives, he admitted he had always had a crush on me. I am thinking, *"Definitely not."* In my mind I saw it coming and thought, "Do not ask me out, please." I just responded, "Aww, that is sweet" and changed the subject. We texted here and there. He let me know when something exciting had happened in his day, such as when a baby calf was born.

There was another guy on the dating site who was very persistent and wanted to meet me. The whole time I was waiting for him, I told myself to call it off, that this was not smart of me. I wanted to, I really did, WHY did I not? Thoughts like, *"What will he think of me; he's already on his way and may get upset with me."* Why, oh why, would I care about what a stranger thought of me! How had I become so reckless with my life that I would be willing to put myself in danger? My life had become far from what used to be a safe little bubble, one that I missed so much. Oh, how I missed that little bubble.

This stranger drove up, and when he got out of his truck I saw that he was a big, strong guy. I invited him in to talk. We sat on the couch, and well, he did not want to talk. He tried to kiss me, and I told him I was not interested in anything like that, that we had planned on talking. He looked at me and said he did not want to talk, and that he thought I like him. I told him I did not know him enough to know that. I tried to delay what I felt was the inevitable. He grabbed me, threw me over his shoulder and walked into the bathroom. I told him multiple times to put me down, and he just laughed as if he thought I was funny. He opened the shower door and put me in there. I tried not to show my fear, but I was scared out of my mind, saying "No, I want out."

After multiple attempts to get out and telling him no, I realized that no was not going to stop him. My thoughts were all over the place and I panicked, *"No one knows he is here. I am all alone, and he's so big and strong."* With that thought, I did what I had to do in order to protect my children's mother…I went into survival mode. I wanted it over with so that he would leave; I stopped fighting and he did what he wanted and left. He acted like it was no big deal and even tried to stay in contact with me afterwards. I ignored all his calls and texts from then on. I never told anyone what had happened, and I blamed myself for the actions that placed me in such a bad situation. I made myself forget his face and his name. Once more, this was something that added to my pile of shame. I felt so dirty that I became one of those girls who say to themselves, *"Who am I; I am nothing."* After all this happened, I found myself scared to death of what I might get myself into. I mean, I had allowed that to happen, then what else would I allow to happen? I did not trust myself at that point anymore.

The next day, my phone rang; it was the other guy (remember my old neighbor?) telling me about his day.

Later in the conversations, he asked me if he could take me out, and I agreed. My thoughts were, *"I trust him; he is safe."* We started dating, and he became just that, my safe place. I trusted him; he was just a good ole boy who had never been married. He knew my story, saw many of my tears and we agreed that we would date for a while. He even said that it takes months to really get to know someone. I relaxed knowing that he felt that way. To my surprise, he proposed a few months later at his parents' home. They were excited and had been waiting for that day for years. At that moment, I was thinking "No, not again, Amy," but I said yes. I loved his family; they were so good to me and my children. I just wanted normal, a family and some structure in my life. Another thing that gave me comfort and a sense of security was that I could sit on his front porch and see the place I had grown up for the first twenty years of my life. I just wanted to be there, back at home. I felt a sense of peace and could feel my daddy there.

As the months went by, his mom and I began planning this BIG wedding. I went to his house to use his computer, and when I moved the mouse the screen opened with the dating website where we had met. Why, why was he on this website? My heart raced. I started breathing faster as I looked at his account and all the messages between him and other women. My heart sank when I saw he had been on there the whole time, talking to someone and that he had NEVER gotten off after we started dating. I was crushed. Pacing around his house questioning everything, I looked in the mirror and told myself I didn't deserve this, but then at the same moment I thought, *"This is probably what I deserve and all that I could get because of my past behavior. I did* not *deserve integrity or honesty because of my lack of those things in the past.*" My heart was broken. I could barely breathe, but knew I had to confront him. I called him to ask about it. He said he was just bored and that's why he was on there. We were engaged, and I was scared and did not have a backbone or self-worth, I just let it go and forgave him. Many more things came up again and again with my heart being broken.

I became so insecure and paranoid, but I stayed. Why? The depths of my heart were screaming at me *"Amy, you do not deserve this! This is nothing but drama and chaos, and this isn't God's best for you."* I responded with these thoughts, *"What! God's best for me? Like I deserve His best. I do not deserve anything but pain and destruction for the rest of my life."* These are the kinds of self-loathing thoughts that filled my mind, and I constantly told myself. I could not forgive myself for anything I had done to my family, and that unforgiveness kept me from seeing my true worth and value in Christ. I was allowing men to treat me badly because that's what I felt I deserved.

We married nine months after we started dating; it was not a good day. I had a meltdown earlier that day. My friend looked at me and said, "I'll take you out the back door right now; you don't have to answer to anyone." Every pore in my body wanted to scream, "YES! Take me!" I could see it playing out in my mind – Julia Roberts in The Runaway Bride; the one thing missing in me from that movie was courage. I quickly reminded myself of his mom, of all the money his family had spent and how this would cause more chaos. It was just easier for my emotions to do it this way and go through with the wedding. I craved his attention, but our wedding night he rejected me, and in my mind I really did not deserve better. I settled for whatever leftovers I could get from him. The first three months after we were married, life was very hard. My new husband was withdrawn, and when I encouraged marriage counseling or maybe doing a marriage study together the lack of emotion from him spoke loud and clear. I longed for Jesus and would seek Him out of desperation but immediately turned away because of shame. I had failed Him, remember?

When I did not have my children, I was a depressed, crying and lifeless mess. It became worse over time. By then I hated myself; I mean I really hated myself. The verbal self-abuse was repetitive. The rejection from my husband did not help. We both knew we had no business getting married, and after a few months he wanted a divorce. I was frantic and desperate to save my marriage. I tried to save it because I did not want another divorce, but it was over. I reached out to someone close to him one day and asked for their advice, explaining that I did not want to lose my marriage. They said, "I think you are the problem, seeing this is husband number three." Those words crushed me; I did not expect those words from this person. We had been close but now it seemed they were attacking me. *"Am I just that dirty that no one has anything good to say of me?"*

That evening as the sun was setting, I stood outside and cried out to God. How and why had this become my life? *"God, I was good for so long. I worked so hard. I chose to be the boring girl just to be sure I did right, did what I was told for so long. Now, my daddy is gone, and this is what has become of me."* There is nothing worse than the feeling of hopelessness →

because in that emotion you can, and will, drive your life right off into a ditch.

# CHAPTER 4

# Maybe, Maybe Not

L ate Summer 2010

After my third divorce, I told my first husband I was going to move back closer to him. I had moved thirty miles away back to my hometown after our divorce. By moving back now we would both be able to be involved with our kids as much as possible. By this time, our kids were seven and three years old; I thought a new start would help. Deep down, my desire was to restore my first marriage and family, but I did not even know where to start or how to go about that. A thought was as far as that went.

I was searching, worried and fearful with not a bit of confidence in myself. It was fall 2010. A friend who was helping me move back knew I was struggling. He told me to look up and read Psalm 37; verse five said,

**Commit your ways to the Lord, trust also in Him,
and He shall bring it to pass.
Psalm 37:5**

*God was speaking to me, right? Could it be that easy?* My thoughts went right to the scripture He had given me over one year earlier while sitting on my front porch, Isaiah 28:21. Could it be? Could I believe Him? You would think that my God moment would last longer than a few minutes, but what was weighing me down was all those bad choices. Just a few seconds of thinking about my past could paralyze me emotionally for days. I went about my new start longing for joy but felt guilty if I was anything but a representative of shame. It was my new identity, and I did not deserve to have anything good in my personal life.

I bought a house and got settled in. I started going back to a church where I had been a member, and I hid in the back. I had NEVER been a backrow Baptist, but that's where I wanted to be, and not be seen. The church knew of my bad choices. Remember, this was a very small town. I began hearing people making comments about me. Those comments drove home the personal thoughts of hatred for myself. I thought, *"If these people do not value me why would God?"* I sat in my shame more and more, and as I did that I wore the Christian mask and tried to fake it. I put on the *"Oh, I'm alright"* look. I carried so much shame and guilt that it clouded my every thought, and I fought it off daily so I could do life. It was easily seen that I ducked my head in order to not make eye contact with those who I thought had their lives together.

As I sat in my mess, the memory of that night's phone

call from a wrong number before my first divorce bubbled up onto the surface. *"Remember, Amy?"* Wow, I didn't think I would ever empathize with the girl that called that night, but I was now her. I just needed to make a call to someone for help BUT I didn't feel like I could do something like that. If I did make a call like that, how would I begin to explain my feelings? I did not even understand me, so how could anyone else understand me? Oh my, that was a lie I believed for years!

I felt so down that I could not even describe the pain and heartache with human language. I could not look at the kids' pictures from the past without having a breakdown that led to just wanting to die. All I had ever wanted in life was to be a godly wife and mom, and I had blown it. I had lost my identity, but then did I really ever have one? The identity I thought I had was grown from self-success and hard work, carbon copied from the life of my daddy…all those years of trying to be the best on MY OWN at the whole wife and mom thing. You see? I did not identify with God's grace and love because my identity was in other people. It took many more wrong roads for me to realize this.

Late in the fall of 2010, I found myself in another relationship. Oh, but I tried. I tried to scare this one off. While checking Facebook on my little BlackBerry phone (which I could barely navigate), I had a friend request from Will. I did not get on Facebook much, but could not sleep that night. I do not accept friend requests from people I do not know (Hey, I was trying to place some boundaries, y'all!). I saw that we had a mutual friend and thought I may have known him from when my first husband and I lived in his town. I looked at his picture and could not place him. I private-messaged him to ask if I knew him from when I lived there. He told me that I did not know him. I explained that I do not accept friend requests from people I do not know but because we had a mutual friend I would accept this time.

It became obvious right away that he was way more interested in getting to know me than I was in getting to know to him. I told him I was a wreck and an emotional basket case. He was so forward about wanting to get to know me more, so I thought, *I know what will scare him off.* I told him I had three prior marriages, thinking that would scare him away. He continued talking to me; I was like, "Hello? Did you just hear me? Married three times!" Because of my own mess, I was thinking, *What is wrong with this guy?* I did enjoy his company, however, and was attracted to the confidence he had in himself, probably because I longed for that confidence in myself.

You would think I would have been banned from marriage after the third one, right? I wish they would have put me on some kind of restriction or even a quarantine! I knew I was not emotionally healthy enough to agree to another relationship, especially not another marriage. Why wouldn't I ever stand up for what I really wanted? I did not want a relationship; what I really needed was a friend. Why was I always pulled and swayed whichever way? I had never been confident enough in myself to self-govern my own life, and that left me vulnerable.

I always adapted to my surroundings for survival, like a chameleon, but I always felt that I did not have a voice.

It seemed that the strongest, most aggressive personality around me at the time was the one that would lead me. How had I become someone who went wherever the wind blew me? I was stuck in quicksand, and when I moved an inch I was sucked back down a foot.

Around this time, I was at work straightening products on one of the aisles, and I heard "Hey." I turned to look, and to my horror, I saw the man who had taken advantage of me over a year ago. I became fearful, and my instinct was to get to the front of the store. As I walked toward the front, he followed me and tried to get me to talk to him. He asked why I was ignoring him. I didn't reply and checked out some customers. He moved to my checkout line, and I continued to ignore him. I only said what was necessary to him, as if he was a customer. He asked me for my phone number, but I refused to give it to him. He finally left. As I continued checking out customers, the phone rang. I quickly answered with a, "Hello, thank you for calling," and I heard, "Why won't you give me your number?" I hung up the phone without saying a word. I was so nervous; I walked to the entrance of the building and could see him in the parking lot. I waited to see what he would do next, but he finally left. I never heard from him again. The incident, however, left me struggling for a few days, having flashbacks and trying to forget what had happened. Again, I was dealing with that past incident on my own in secret.

Will continued to become more and more serious about me, and one day I popped off to him, "Please do not fall in love with me and do not ask to marry me." He probably thought I was full of myself already, saying DO

NOT MARRY ME. In fact, I was the complete opposite, not full at all but very empty. I was hoping that he would just slow down and hang out with me after hearing the mess I had been through. He had already been told I was not capable of a relationship and was borderline insane (doing the same thing repeatedly, expecting a different result). He was seeing just how lonely and depressed I was when I did not have my kids. I told him, "I just want my kids all the time." He knew the guilt I carried. He knew I felt like a failure as a mom; I made it clear. I did not hide anything; I told him up front that I was not emotionally stable.

A few weeks later, Will proposed. Seriously, the room felt like it was closing in on me as he asked me to marry him. Everything inside of me wanted to say, "Not now," but I said yes. My thoughts were everywhere from *"I do not want this – not now"* to *"Well I'm here so maybe it'll be something stable in my life."* I did not want to hurt his feelings. He may have been ready for marriage, but I was not. Will was going to take me to Vegas six weeks after that for a getaway and wanted to get married while we were there. He assured me that I did not have to if I did not want to. Hey, I knew me well enough to know that if I was not being pushed into doing something, I would not do it. Therefore, I knew I would probably not go through with it.

Right before we left, I found out I was pregnant, which only added to the stress and emotions of everything else that was going on. I had the flu on top of it all. I was so sick. It was time for the ceremony, and I could not go through with it. As I stood in the bathroom looking at myself, I knew I could not do it. I was just strong enough to utter those words to Will. He was not happy; his response was shocking as I had never seen that kind of reaction from him before. I was a mess, crying, hyperventilating, panicking all at the same time and then went numb when Will expressed his emotions in ways that triggered painful past responses. I immediately put walls up, shut down and remained quiet.

I was standing in front of the big picture window of our hotel room, tears and mascara running down my face onto the silk purple top I was wearing. My mind was so overloaded with emotions from all the wrong choices that had led me to that very moment. I felt as if my mind was drowning in it all. My heart was so heavy that I felt as if it would fall right out of my body. I felt helpless, *"Here I go again! How does this keep happening?"* It seemed that I had no say or control over my life. All I could say was that I wanted my kids, and I was tired of making wrong choices.

In Will's anger brought on by what I was telling him, he told me if we were not getting married that I had to have an abortion. Oh wait, here is the only moment I used to climb on my soap box! "I am not killing my baby," I said frantically. To me, that was the last little bit of dignity I had left to stand for. I may have screwed up in so many other ways, but do not tell me to get an abortion. After about an hour of the emotional battle, I finally gave in and gave up. Why fight for myself? I felt I did not deserve the effort, and apparently no one else thought highly enough of me to give me a voice. The mental and emotional block that had been erected in my mind was layered thick and sky high.

Will and I said our vows as I stood there like a pillar, putting on a smile long enough to get away with making him happy. We headed home the next day, and on the plane ride home I remember sitting there feeling myself sink into a very low, dark and restless place. This was a new low for me; I had never felt the depths of this lowly feeling. Will saw it happening before his eyes; he saw the blank, emotionless stare on my face. In that moment, I just wanted to die. I did not want to feel the shame that covered me like thick mud anymore or the guilt that oozed out of every pore in my body.

The next few weeks were a rollercoaster ride. I felt good one day and deeply depressed the next. I was good as long as my kids were with me, but as soon as they left to go to their dad's I retreated into my hole. One day it was just too much for me to bear. I could not bear one more moment of the thoughts in my head. I wanted to not feel at all. With a chest tight with panic, I grabbed my phone and sent a text to Will as fast as I could, "I do not want this, please leave me alone."

I just needed it all to go away. I could not handle my emotions. I shut him out along with everyone else. He tried to contact me, but when he did what he said was not nice. I knew he was angry and hurt, but what he said about me over the phone dug deep into a place I had not seen, the lowest of lows. I took a walk into a lifeless and yet again another unknown territory.

I sat on the back porch of my friend, Jamie's, house. I hung up the phone from what was the most chaotic conversation, and it only pushed me farther overboard. So much had been done and said; I looked at Jamie and said, "I will do what he wants me to do." Yes, I was talking about an abortion. She knew this was not like me. Something in me snapped! The little bit of self-worth I may have had somewhere deep within was now gone. I had removed myself from myself, if that makes sense. I had no feelings or emotions. I had to do that because of what I was agreeing to do.

As I Googled listings for abortions clinics, I was doing so with the one thought, *"This is the only way."* I was not mentally strong enough to handle this mess. I called somewhere in Texas first to ask about an abortion. *Did I just really call and ask for that?* It was like there were two of me, as though part of me was out of my body watching the actions and words from the other part. The lady on the phone said they would have to refer me to another clinic because they did not perform abortions there. Each time I heard the word "abortion" or had to say the word, a chill raced up and down my spine.

I called an abortion clinic in Shreveport, Louisiana known as Hope Medical for Women. I set up an appointment for a few days later. It was explained to me over the phone that it is required by law to have an ultrasound prior to having the abortion. I guess the politicians sleep better at night after passing that law. As I was driving to my ultrasound appointment, I had convinced myself I was doing this and that there were no other options. In my mind, my mess was far from ever being repairable.

I drove up to the back of the abortion building. *"Am I here?"* I thought. I kept telling myself, *"There is just no other way. I've already hurt my other kids with breaking up their family and they need me."* I had so much focus on giving to my kids in every way because I felt I had destroyed their home. This was not what I had in mind. This was not perfect. It was all too much, plus Will did not want the baby. I was one nerve away from ending my life. *"If only I had the guts to do it"* I thought. I loved my kids too much to end my life, but I did think about it a lot.

So here I was, sitting at a place I never thought I would be. I was getting ready to get out of my car when I looked over to my right. There stood an older man facing the street. I saw him there, but he had not seen me. *"Oh no,"* I thought, *"of course there would be someone there. It's an abortion clinic, Amy you know what this place is."* I looked at him again, and now he was looking right at me. I put my head down in shame. I was thinking, *"I cannot go in with him looking at me. He knows why I'm here."* He stood there holding a rosary. I saw his sweet face, and I could see the heaviness of his heart for me. I knew he was praying for me because I saw his mouth moving and I felt the Holy Spirit moving inside of my walled-up heart. He finally turned away, and I ran inside.

I opened a heavy, brown metal door and walked into a dungeon lit up by fluorescent lights. The smell of the mold from the moldy old floors and ceilings stank. I sat there waiting to be called back, knowing that I could not watch this mandatory ultrasound. Sitting next to me was a very young girl, and her leg was shaking. She was so nervous, and in a split second I thought, *"She is here to kill her baby."* I quickly realized my emotions had come back to the surface, and I went back into shutdown mode. As I awaited my turn, I picked up a booklet that shared things about why it may not be the right timing to have a baby and other reasons that abortion is the best option. I found myself reading each page, and with each word pouring into my heart, abortion was made to sound normal and pleasant. I bought the lie. I thought to myself, *"They understand why I must do this. It is alright."*

But it was so twisted.

That is why it is important to be careful of what we read, what goes into our minds and hearts. I read a poem about killing the unborn and that even sounded okay to me at that point.

My name was called; it was time. I followed the lady to the ultrasound room and got up onto the table. A gray-haired lady did the ultrasound. I told her there was just no way I could look, and she said, "Do not worry, sweetheart, you do not have to." I lay there as she applied gel to my stomach and then glided the ultrasound probe along. She said I was measuring at thirteen weeks. I thought, *"Why is she talking to me about this?"* I asked her to please not tell me anything. I could not handle the reality of what I was doing; it was all I could do to keep my "do not feel" mindset.

Afterwards, I was taken to a room with bi-fold doors where I saw a TV. I was told I had to watch a video of the abortion procedure. What! "NO!" I said with a loud voice, "I CANNOT WATCH THAT! I cannot do it." Again, the nurse said I did not have to watch. I was taken to talk to the so-called "doctor" who asked why I was choosing an abortion. "I cannot do this," I said. "I cannot handle all that is going on in my life." I was a mess, and he saw that. He asked how many kids I had, and I told him two. His exact words to me were, "Oh, two are plenty." I will never forget how easy it was for him to say that. As I stepped outside his office to leave, I looked to the left down the hall where it opened at the back to a bigger room. A lady was gathering up blue medical pads, and I saw blood on them. I felt a cold chill sweep over my whole body. *"Oh my gosh, oh my gosh.... Block it out Amy, block this out!"*

My abortion appointment was made for the next Thursday. I asked my friend Jamie if she would take me, and she refused to be a part. I was so out of it, and in complete desperation I told her if she would not go then I would find someone off the street to go with me. It was as if my body was on autopilot. I had a one-track mind at this point. I see now how far someone can go with uncontrolled thoughts and where those thoughts can take them (Remember just the week prior I was on my soap box saying I was not going to kill my baby! How dare someone ask me to do such a thing!) After my crazy threat, Jamie agreed to go with me to the clinic. I picked her up from work, and in her hand she had pages with pictures that showed what my baby's stages of development would be.

For the next twenty miles, Jamie never took a breath. She reminded the Amy that was tucked away deep inside of what that Amy believed, and THAT Amy was against abortion. I was zoned out with my hands firmly gripping the steering wheel, *"do not think or feel"* was what I was repeating to myself. On the Loop in Carthage, it was like a dark cloud lifted from me, and I snapped out of it. I cried out, "I CANNOT KILL MY BABY!"

Jamie replied, "Praise God!" I quickly pulled over. I started crying and said, "What kind of person am I? I was going to kill my own baby! The very same baby I was singing to and talking to weeks earlier." How does someone get to that kind of place so quickly, a place they would've never seen for themselves. This seemed to be a repeating problem in my life.

Even though the abortion did not happen, I was still not taking care of myself. I was not eating much and was not gaining weight. Weeks later, I had lab work done and was told the results showed there was a possibility that my baby would have Down Syndrome. They would later be able to tell for sure by ultrasound. After hanging up from that phone call, guilt came over me. I thought this was, in some way, punishment for almost taking my baby's life. Weeks later, and with Jamie by my side, they first said, "IT'S A GIRL!" Then, they said there were no signs that she would be born with Down Syndrome.

As the weeks passed, I was still in "blah mode", or that's what I called it. All I wanted was to be around my kids; when I was with them I felt peace to make life bearable. They were the only good thing of me I had left, and what little purpose I had left was being their mom. I could not be alone because being alone with my thoughts scared me. I began to hang out at their dad's house to be near them; I felt safe there. The remnants of home I had left were there, and I felt peace there. I looked around and was reminded of all I had lost; it left me more and more confused. How could I have done all that? I had no answers. How does someone who was happy with life just throw it away so fast? I'd never had impulsive behavior before, so what caused it? The questions lingered so long that they physically hurt my body. I was a broken woman both physically and mentally, a sad waste of a once-blessed life.

I was sitting on the couch at twenty-four weeks along in my pregnancy, although I looked to be more like twelve weeks' pregnant. I thought, *"Did I just wet myself?"* I ran to the bathroom, and sure enough my water had broken. I drove myself to the hospital, and my momma met me there. I was quickly given a steroid shot that felt as if a knife stabbed my hip. I had no insurance, so the hospital to which I was being transferred would not accept me. I was told I would have to go to another hospital. Momma begged and pleaded with the doctor and asked him to reconsider. Within moments, the hospital changed their minds. My doctor said, "Amy, someone must be watching out for you because this hospital does not change its mind." Soon after, I was transferred by ambulance to Christus Schumpert in Shreveport, Louisiana, the best place for preemies to be born.

I was in good hands, yet, as all of this was going on I was so out of it, just numb, on autopilot. Every part of me wanted to feel again and be present in the moment, but when I began to feel, I could not cope with it all. I would shut down again because I could not handle "feelings;" they were just too much for me. The ONLY relief I felt was when I saw my kids; they distracted me from the heartache, and they were the only things keeping me from ending my life at that point.

For eight long days, I was on bed rest in the hospital. I could not shower or walk. My hair was so oily that I could have made a sculpture with it, but at this point in my life I could not have cared less. The only thing on television at that time was the movie Spiderman. I think I probably hold some sort of record for watching that. Momma was there with me most of the time; I told her to go home and get some rest and PLEASE do not tell Will that I was there. In my anger towards him I had become selfish about telling him anything about the pregnancy. I was still covered in hopelessness as I lay there in that labor and delivery room for eight days. I was alive on the outside but felt dead and dark on the inside.

On Sunday morning, Father's Day, June 19, 2011, I woke up feeling very ill; my body felt chilled and weak. I rolled over and looked behind me at the monitor that usually showed mine and the baby's heart rate. The screen was black and blank except for a scripture. I thought, *"Could God be speaking to me? Could He? What does that scripture even mean?"* I quickly ignored it because I told myself I did not deserve the love that He spoke of. It was almost like a false sense of hope that I wanted no part of. I had developed an infection, and with that, my fever was high, so they had to induce labor. It all happened so quickly. Doors flew open, medical equipment was brought into my room and set up to care for a little baby. I did not have time to think about the risks that I had already been told about days earlier from the doctor because the contractions had become more and more intense. My mom was not present, and I needed her! I had no one. I was alone, just as I felt on the inside.

There was no time for pain medication. I screamed with every contraction. *"This is labor,"* I thought. I had been given pain relief with my other deliveries, so this pain was eye-opening. I was being a wimp, screaming and moaning at every contraction. One nurse came over and said to me in a snotty tone, "You have got to stop being so loud! We can hear you all over the unit and you are going to upset the other patients." Most women might have told her where to go in that moment, but in my shame I thought, *"Even she knows I do not deserve kindness and care."* Even in my pain I felt like a scolded child thinking, "Oh gosh, I have upset someone."

I tried so hard with the next contraction not to scream; then, just like that God sent this sweet, blue-eyed angel nurse to my side. She held my hand and told me to focus on her. I will never forget how she stepped in and made me feel like it was all right to show how and what I was going through. I heard the nurse say, "Oh no, meconium." I knew that was bad, and it had not happened with my other deliveries.

Then, it was over, and out came a little baby girl. Bright spotlights blurred my vision; I could not see her as they took her to the heated bed and surrounded her with emergency equipment. Nurses and doctors gathered around her fragile little body as they did what they do best – save babies. I was so scared to look at her for many reasons: I had almost killed her, I was not taking care of myself, I could not give her the life I wanted to give her. How could I face her without more shame and guilt? They were still working on her; I heard one of them say, "She's a kicker."

They stabilized her, rolled her out the door, and said it was all right to look. I pulled myself up to see her tiny arms and legs moving all around. She was so tiny but looked just like a full-term baby but with smaller features. I felt emotions again, love rushing over me for her, but I also felt guilt. The nurses asked me what I was going to name her, but I had not even picked one for her. I wanted her to have one right then because she deserved one. Right from that Spiderman movie I had watched so many times came the name "Emma," I told them, "and by the grace of God, she is here and will live. Emma Grace."

## CHAPTER 5

# Let's Try This Again

Days later I was released from the hospital, but Emma stayed. My friend Jamie told me that she had made an appointment with a counselor for me.

I told the counselor where I was at that moment, that Emma was in the hospital, that I had gone through a divorce and was drowning in shame. I did not tell her about any of my other marriages, my childhood or my other inner personal struggles. I was still in denial about most of my issues. After hearing what little I said, the counselor said, "Do you know that God has empathy for you?" When she said that, it was like for just a moment I gave myself permission not to showcase my past anymore, showcase being the key word because I stored it in my back pocket from then on.

With my one and only counseling session under my belt, I thought I had this guilt and shame thing beat, but it was all just a mirage. Hearing God had empathy for me gave me a boost to be headed in the right direction, but I was very naïve as to the depths of my wounds.

A few days had passed. I unblocked Will's phone number and sent him a text that simply read, "She is beautiful, isn't she?" We met at the hospital later that week to be with Emma. The nurses looked at me like, "Okay." I am sure they were confused about what I said a few days earlier, "I do not want to be around her dad at all, so make sure he is not here when I come to see her." Between the chaos in my personal life and my all-over-the-place hormones, I may have been a bit dramatic with that. I thought all would be great now because I was not sitting in that black hole anymore. In reality, I was faking this new chapter in hopes I could fool even myself, rainbows and sparkles I would say.

Will and I were getting to know each other better and started to build some foundation from what we once were. We continued to see Emma together. As our relationship grew, we decided to get back together (we had not divorced while we were separated). As the weeks went by, I guess the "high" of being back together faded. One day out of the blue, Will brought up some of the past things I had done, and there I stood face to face with IT. The IT being my past. IT was staring me down with its evil grin. It was laughing at me as I willingly allowed it back in. It very slowly began to pick away at my wounds. I felt that dirty, guilty feeling begin to flood over me once again. I felt as if I had shrunk to the depths of one inch in height; my shoulders fell, my head to the ground. I remembered those feelings from months before: dirty, ashamed, guilty, and feeling worthless and hopeless. I tried to hold onto the words spoken to me by the counselor before, that God had empathy for me. Who was I kidding? I felt that I would never be anything but the mistakes I had made. I found myself crying out to God to reassure me, but I found myself longing for man's approval instead of God's. His voice always seemed to be drowned out by the enemy's reminders.

*"No! This was supposed to be my start-over, the new chapter after living in shame for so long. No God, why?"* The negative words said to me by Will were later followed up by nice words, but the ones I repeated over and over in my mind were the negative words. It was a repetitive unhealthy cycle that had grown as the years had gone by. I did not speak of that verbal abuse or the chaos to anyone. When negative moments unfolded after that, I found myself looking for an exit window, a door, anything. It did not matter where I was, when those moments occurred I always looked for a place to run, and I did.

Will had a daughter from a previous marriage. Neither of our houses were big enough for all six of us, so we sold our houses and bought a house that would fit us all. The most important thing to me was being a mom. I was devoted to always being present and available to each of my children, including my stepdaughter. I did what I do best; I was the peacekeeper, oh and let's not forget a great housekeeper! I did not know how to protect my kids from hearing the yelling and negative things in our home. I mean, I was grown and couldn't handle those things myself. I had extreme panic and anxiety for them and felt helpless about how to shield them from those things. I always tried to control what I could and to make sure that nothing caused problems. Here

I was, feeling like the child I was with my parents, trying to control my surroundings and outcomes.

I tried to be ten steps ahead of everything. *Maybe if I just love Will enough, he will be happy. Maybe the problem was with me.* He doesn't treat anyone else like this. I thought maybe if I was more outgoing, if I talked more, if I was skinnier, then maybe he would treat me better. I began focusing on my outer appearance, since I had not focused on it much before. I was always good with the outer me; that was the only thing I hadn't attacked yet. I started trying to become "better." *"If I am better, he will be happier!"* I entered the Mrs. Texas pageant and competed for four years. I was attempting to change me to receive approval from him, as well as others, but it seemed that my past was always just around the next corner.

When I felt I was moving forward, something would pop up. Upon entering the Mrs. Texas pageant, all contestant names and photos were placed on their webpage. One morning I woke up to look at the webpage, and to my shock (but not really) some people from my past had posted some negative things about me. I felt overwhelmed and panicked, seeing the comments there for the whole world to see. Everything inside of me wanted to quit right then and there. It seemed my past was always laughing at me. I messaged the state director; at that moment I felt I was the only one with a messy past and did not deserve to compete. The directors said that it was all right, and she removed the negative comments. Somewhere in my head I thought the pageant would ask me to step down; I had convinced myself that I was the only broken woman competing.

So, let's talk PAGEANT for a moment. At that

time, I was reaching for fulfillment and acceptance from whatever source I could find. This was only one of the many distractions I used to keep my mind off the real issues, and it WORKED. I was probably the most out-of-place contestant at the pageant; this became apparent on more than one occasion. For example, when we all went out to eat the night after orientation, I ordered chicken fried steak and mashed potatoes. As I looked around the table, I saw that everyone else had ordered SALADS! Oh really, Amy, how embarrassing (but not as embarrassing as wearing that red bikini for the photo shoot earlier in the day)!

One of the girls who was not competing but there to support a friend, sat beside me at dinner; she said to me "You're brave eating that! I'm impressed to see a pageant girl eating like that." I had been starving myself for weeks, but looking at this plate of comfort food, I dug right in. I knew it didn't matter. What was a little water retention compared to my broken life? I felt that these women were way more put together than I was or ever could be. I was just the washed-up version of the woman I used to be, soaking wet, each drop consisting of guilt and shame.

Throughout the pageant weekend I was thinking to myself, *"Why am I here? I don't belong."* These thoughts were even stronger as I stood in front of the judges for my interview. As I went into that interview room, a woman told me to just relax and be myself. Yeah, I thought, *"Could you please tell me who that may even be?"* There I stood in front of the panel of judges; they were all very professional-looking and successful people. I was overwhelmed with fear. My legs were shaking, and feet ached from my very uncomfortable high heels. I thought, *"I'm not good enough to be here. I've probably been married more times than all their marriages put together and have a sixth-grade education. You're a joke. Be myself. Really? I don't even look like myself."* I had enough makeup on to paint the ceiling of a cathedral in a Catholic church, and I won't even talk about my spray tan. Was this a pageant or a body-building competition?

Throughout each part of the pageant, I was not me, or even acting like myself. One particular moment of the competition took my breath away, but in a good way. As I put my evening gown on and looked into the mirror, I felt like a princess; it was more like a Cinderella moment. The ten-pound beaded gown had, in just one zip, covered a lot of unseen shame and guilt. All I needed was that Mrs. Texas crown, right? When the light from the stage reflected off the jewels from the dress, the reflection lit up the stage; that was my "Amy doesn't feel as dirty and shameful" moment. As I write this now, my heart breaks for the thirty-two year-old woman who was struggling inside.

The top twelve were announced, but I didn't make the cut. I was top thirteen. I went backstage and cried, not even sure why I was. I thought, *"Why on earth am I crying?"* Then, the words I secretly whispered to myself over the past few years began to bubble back to the surface through all the makeup and pretty stuff: *"Rejection, insignificance, not good enough, I let my kids down. It's because you've been divorced before. You've made too many mistakes to ever deserve a crown."*

I pulled myself together and swept all that back under the rug where it belonged, and I began to cheer on my new friends. I went home afterward and thought that was the end of pageants for me. BUT THEN, a thought and challenge came to my mind. *What if I became just like the rest of them?* This meant I would have to change my whole look and spend crazy amounts of money, and so it began. I grew my hair out, added extension, joined a gym, paid for a personal trainer and someone to teach me how to walk and talk. Yeah, that's crazy, right? It's like I was a toddler again. I was told to break speaking habits such as, "and things like that, y'all, and fixin' to," which was a bit challenging. If I could just *not* be ME, if I could just be someone else, someone to cover up the real me. All those "pretty things" and "self-focus" created even more self-destruction.

About this same time, a friend reached out to me and wanted us to get together for a play date for our kids so we could get to know each other better. I began to have anxiety about having to tell her my past because I thought she needed to know up front what a screw-up I was. I did not have any friends at this time, so I felt this would be good. She later told me she was "warned" about me. Warned? I did not understand why others were talking about me. In my mind, this was just verification that I was worthless. It was hard for me to put myself out there to this lady who wanted to get to know me. The things I had been telling myself for all those years were now ringing in my ears. I had messed up, and I would be forever broken. It seemed I was under a microscope, and it was probably because of my very messy past. I felt like I was just not liked and was being picked apart. I did not understand what was different about me and other people except for my publicly known past mistakes. Did they not know that their words and actions toward me only clarified how I felt about myself, adding wounds and nail holes to my façade. They did not understand that I, myself, was once just like them, high and mighty on my pedestal looking at what I could never be. The shame and guilt that I thought I had under control was placed in my back pocket, although I would pull it out from time to time to soak myself in it. I was reminded of my past constantly. No matter what I did, I could not get away from it.

When my marriage was good, it was very good, but when it was bad it was very bad. Then, I would shut down emotionally because it was exhausting. Shut-down mode was my safe place; if I did not have to feel anything it did not hurt as badly. Will and I began getting involved in our community. It was easy for Will to socialize; he was a people person and never met a stranger. He became friends with others easily. As for me, I would be all right living on a secluded mountain ALONE with a few goats. There were some people who were planning a trip together, and Will and I also planned to go. I already felt like I did not belong, but when we were "uninvited" to go on the trip, it confirmed to me that it was because of me and my past. I felt I was the problem, and at that time I even wondered if they had been told about all my marriages and my almost-abortion. Will had not been told about my trip to the abortion clinic yet. It was hard to feel worthy of anything in my life when I felt so dirty and rejected by others around me. Wallowing in that feeling of worthlessness, I pushed myself into isolation. Where there is isolation, there is darkness, and darkness breeds ugly things.

The verbal and emotional abuse in our marriage continued for almost four years. I never told anyone (not even Momma who would've been heartbroken), because of embarrassment and fear. This is what I thought I deserved for myself. It was hard for me to accept that I could enjoy life, that I was worthy to be treated with respect, but I felt I was not worthy of joy or peace. Chaos is what enslaved me. I prayed and tried to move closer to God, but the words were just that, words. I did not believe that I deserved all the things I read in the Bible or heard preachers speak about. I felt God had abandoned me at times. *"God, where are you?"* I cried out at night in my prayers. I still mourned the loss of my family. It was hard sorting through the emotions that divorce creates. I missed my kids so much.

When I tried to work on my marriage with Will I felt it was wrong because I did not deserve happiness; the situations in our marriage seemed to validate that point. My thoughts were that I had made my bed and these were the consequences of my first divorce. With all that being said, God designed marriage as a way for protection, safety, wholeness, and togetherness of family. God does not want moms and dads to miss out on what He has planned for them in His perfect will. Because of my divorce and children living with their daddy fifty percent of the time, there were nights of empty beds, and I missed out on tucking my babies into their beds.

It was all a heart and mind battle, and I felt defeated. *"How could this be my life,"* I asked myself daily. Not knowing how to cope, I learned to push down my feelings and emotions even deeper. I had no one to talk to; I was lonely and empty. If someone listened, they would get an earful because I needed to be heard, but I suffered in secret. My sleep and body were affected by the never-ending chaos in our home and in my mind.

Because of low self-esteem, I became jealous with everything to do with Will: his work, his employees, his hobbies, and his ex-wife. I was jealous because I wanted to have what they got from him. The jealously grew into a huge monster that I tried to keep contained, but it showed up in the weirdest of places. Will had hired a young lady, and I had a panic attack when I found out she had the office beside his. I mean, I had a full-out emotional breakdown; I felt like I couldn't even breathe. I found myself sitting on the tailgate of my truck trying to explain to him why I was so jealous. I told him that I had become an emotional basket case because of the way he treated me and how many of the things produced jealousy in me. He looked at me and said, "What problem? Our marriage is great!" Really! At that time, I felt hopeless as I tried to get him to understand me, and I wanted to pull my hair out.

I stayed focused on being a devoted wife, and even though it was very unstable at times, I never thought about giving up. Nevertheless, the walking on eggshells, the yelling and the chaos pushed me into a place where I began to grow bitter toward him. I grabbed at everything I could to help fill the void and hide the pain. I felt I could not make him happy and that I was not good enough. Soon I snapped, as if someone had flipped a switch in me. I was putting a wall around my heart, and honestly, it was relaxing in that moment not to have to worry about "feeling."

One night while lying in the bed, I asked God "Why?" I had done things the way I felt He wanted me to, but I was still a doormat to Will. I had prayed and had been "faking it until I made it" and never fought back. I was faithful and devoted, but there was still no change. My one last hope was a marriage seminar hosted by Kirk Cameron, which was going to be in Dallas, Texas in November 2013. I soaked up all the information, praying that Will did too. On the way home, I was dying to talk about all we had heard, but instead was met with silence. Will commented that we were fine. It was almost like the last little bit of hope died inside of me, and I saw how delusional he was toward these major issues in our marriage. The only good thing that came out of that trip was meeting Kirk. I was done and had made up my mind on the way home not even to try anymore. All my efforts were wasted anyway. I was tired and had nothing left to give.

Over the next few days, bitterness grew even more toward Will for all that he had said and done in our home. It was too much for me to handle. I had never reached out for help because of my shame. All the suppressed emotions and feelings came at once, but I didn't say a word. I closed and walled up my heart; I thought Will did not care about it anyway. I still tried to be the peacekeeper; remember, I was trained at a very early age to be one. The anxiety and stress I had wore me down. I was having headaches and dizziness that put me on the floor. I was headed down a road to losing my mind; I needed help! *God, where are you??*

I was at home one day with Emma. We were dancing around; I hopped a step and immediately felt the worst stabbing pain in my back. I just knew I had messed up big time. I later found out that I had two herniated discs and posted on Facebook about possibly having to have back surgery. A friend of Will's who lived about four hours away saw my post; he messaged me about his back issues and surgery. He was thoughtful, and I was hungry for kind words. I soaked them up like a dry sponge. This was the beginning of our conversations, and he was an ear to listen as I poured out words of pain. I justified my actions because of Will's actions. Isn't that what we do? "Well, because they did this, I can do that." The infection started and began to spread.

At first, it was innocent, this guy checking on me, but it soon led to me telling him all about my struggles. I told him everything I had ever done and everything that was going on in my home. At first, it was refreshing having someone who would listen to me. It was as though loads of anxiety fell from me in the comfort of his attention. Satan will supply our heart's desires, won't he?

**"But every man is tempted,**
**When he is drawn away of his own lust, and enticed."**
**James 1:4**

At first I said, "You can be the brother I do not have." A week later I said, "You remind me of my daddy." He also shared with me what he had gone through as a child. At that moment, an emotional bond was formed with him because of his pain. Yes, our bond was formed because of our personal pain. I thought, *He needs me; I am going to help him.* I felt badly for him and he did for me. He seemed to care; he spoke kind words to me. I knew I should not be talking to him, and I even told him we could not talk anymore because that is what happened in my first marriage. I did not want to be out of God's will.

After I said I would not be contacting him anymore, I went to bed and cried. The pain from letting those daily conversations go was hard on me. *"God, I know, I see, I get it! I got into another situation, God, and I am so weak."* If I had had any wisdom at all, I would have run to someone who could mentor and counsel me. I was spiritually weak, and Satan knew it. I was facing all of it alone. Again, stupid me could not see that I had opened a box of added issues, and I did not have the foundation to stand and fight them off.

For about a day we did not talk, but then he messaged me to say that he had to talk to me. When I saw the message I was upset because I really was trying to cut off communication with him, but I was craving kindness and would have taken it from anyone at that point. Because I was weak, I caved in at the temptation. Honestly, I did not put up a fight; I was like an addict craving a fix. His words gave me a sense of confidence. His words built me up and made me feel valuable. With that feeling, I was able to take a stand for me. With this newfound confidence I had found in another man, I began to hold my head high. Will could see I was not backing down like I had in the past. He even said that he saw this newfound confidence. With this new confidence that was not from Christ, I ignored Will completely.

I told Will that I was finished and that I wanted him to move out; I really needed to breathe. I remember the peace I had that first night. I felt I had the freedom to relax, and I slept good for the first time in years. It was the same freedom I dreamt about as a kid under my daddy's roof. No more trying to please Will. The house was calm, peaceful and there was no anxiety.

I did not even try to hide my new relationship, and within days Will found out about the other man. Will contacted him and asked him to leave me alone so that he could work on his marriage. I told Will I had feelings for this guy. FEELINGS. What a word. Using that word caused me more heartache! I continued to have an adulterous relationship with that man for about a month after Will moved out.

By this time, Will had started going to a local cowboy church and really became involved. He called and told me all about it, and I rolled my eyes. This was a first, seeing him like this, wanting to be a part of a church. That hurt so much because I had wanted him to choose God when we were together. Why now? One Sunday, Will came back to our church to get re-baptized; he wanted our pastor to do it. He had rededicated his life to Christ. I agreed to be there because I was happy that he was headed down the right path; however, as it turned out I was unable to go because Emma and I were sick that day. I was lying on the couch, and Will came over to the house to check on Emma. While he was there, he brought a wet washcloth and laid in on my forehead. I was so upset; why was he choosing this now after I had asked him to moveout? It was as if a piece of the hard shell had fallen away because of his kind gesture. I was afraid. I thought *"I do not want to put myself into a place to get hurt again,"* but my heart was opening and I was feeling again. I wanted my family but wanted things to be different.

Will went on his way, and the Holy Spirit continued to work on me. My deep desire was always for God, but self was always fighting to do things the world's way.

One night, I took a step back into God's will and told Him I would trust that He was working in my marriage, and I tried to have the faith I needed to move forward with my family being restored. Everything that needed to be worked on was just swept right back under the rug again. *"No! Where was the counseling, the talking it out?"* I saw that things were not going to be resolved, so I just let it be. No talking about things, absolutely nothing. We just reset the timer once again.

## CHAPTER 6

# Second Time's A Charm, Right? Or Third?

I was excited that we had once again figured it out because it was my desire to have my family, minus the chaos.

Will had visited that nearby cowboy church when we were separated, and he really loved it. He asked if I wanted to visit, and I agreed. This was something new, Will engaged in the church and wanting to be involved. God had used our breakup to work in his heart. I knew we would grow and thrive; that was my hope anyway. We went together on a Wednesday night, and of course my social anxiety was through the roof. Look, I would rather dig ditches than walk into a group of people I do not know. I have always had trouble in big groups, and I wanted to hide under a rock. I was never comfortable around people my age; I did not know how to socialize with them. However, if you were my parents' age, then it was no problem. I went to the small women's group that night and really enjoyed it. Someone saw me sticking out like a sore thumb and made me feel at ease because I was new. I fell in love with their concept on outreach, so we joined the church.

Someone there knew I was a singer, and they asked me if I would like to join the band. I thought that would be a good way to use my talent. It was very different at first because I had been singing with soundtracks, not a band. They asked what key I needed for a song, and I laughingly said, "The key of Z." I had no clue. A few months later, I received a Facebook message and was asked to take a break from the band. With everything in me, I tried not to let it affect me, but it did. *Why did I get removed? Was it because of my past? I'm just not worth anything, not even there. Why? Did someone tell them I had been married multiple times? Just give me a scarlet letter to wear!*

I continued to pour myself into pageants each year, working at it and stressing over myself. It was not fun as a hobby should be. A lot of time and money was wasted with little to no benefit. I tried to blend in at church, but I didn't really allow myself to become close with anyone. Getting close to anyone meant that I would have to tell them everything about my past, and I feared rejection. If someone tried to get to know me, I thought I had to pour my past out in that very moment so that they would know who I really was. I just wanted to get it over with. That way, if they thought badly about my past, they would know up front and could choose whether I was friend material.

Our marriage was not as bad as it had been the first four years, but there were still times of yelling and anger. It seemed that I could not do anything right and had anxiety from not knowing when Will would become angry. I would hold in my pain until night-time. I put the kids to bed and then would go into the bathroom and cry. There were many nights I would sit in the bathtub crying out to God, *"Why? Why is it so hard? Please, God, fix this…I am tired of feeling worthless, tired of the panic attacks, tired of having anxiety."*

These things crushed me to the point that I ran! I'd run into the closet or wherever I could find peace. Will is a loud person, and when he was upset he was even louder. In those moments, I wanted to get away and instinctively searched for my car keys or a way to sneak out of the house to leave. I looked for a door or another room to go into. I was not a fighter. I did not have the confidence to stand up and say, "Who do you think you're talking to?" All I wanted was peace. I was so tired of having to please people, and the result was never "rainbows and sparkles" anyway, no matter how bright I tried to make the situation.

If Will and I were at home together, it was very tense at times. I knew he had his own struggles; my silence triggered his, and in return his triggered mine. In those moments, I would ask for us to go to counseling, but he refused. One night when sitting in the bathroom crying, I asked God to take me home if my marriage was never going to change. I was mentally exhausted from the battle inside my head. I could not deal with the agony inside me. I could not take the stress anymore. One night as I showered I realized that I was in a place of being so vulnerable and hungry for peace that I could be tempted to stray yet again.

I was weary and worn out both mentally and physically. I needed a protector because that is how I had always coped with things in my life. It was never sexual attention I longed for. It was always someone to shield me from the pain. Emotionally, I was bone dry; there was nothing there. My prayers turned into whining and complaining about what I did not have in my marriage and in my life. I felt like I was nothing, as if I was a glorified doormat and that was it. My kids were my only joy and comfort.

Instead of allowing God to fill what was a void, I turned back to the world for quick fixes: pageants, singing, photography and whatever else I could do to keep my mind off reality. I had not been involved in Bible studies at church anymore because I helped clean up after Wednesday night meals. Busy is what I did best. Avoid reality and the feelings that hurt me. Just be numb; I was good at that. At this time, I was back with the band full time for just a few weeks. I had conversations with others on Facebook about end times and politics, which kept me preoccupied from the pain of my reality. When I was occupied with other things, I did not have to feel the pain from the things in my life. Those things fed some of my voids. I had become bitter towards Will because we did not have a relationship, and really nothing ever was healed from our past. I hid the bitterness with my smile and rainbow and sparkles sayings, but the pain was still there, a gaping wound. All the hurts and pains that were swept under the rug all bubbled up to the top. When Will would get upset, he brought up past events, and that created in me the attitude of "so be it." I did not care what I allowed into my life anymore.

If that was how it was to be, I was finished crying about me and him anymore. It became very intense at the house. My feelings had become numb, and that always was a bad place to be. I was exhausted from the trying and the faking at life. Will saw that I was shutting down again. My attitude was his tough luck, which was such a snotty attitude, but I was DONE. He then asked about counseling. Oh yeah, he always started to care when I'm so far gone. I told him no. I had one foot out the door but wanted my family; that's what kept me there.

One Sunday morning, all the whining and moaning about what I did not have walked into the doors of our church. It was the beginning of the darkest, scariest road I have ever traveled. I was at early morning band practice before the Sunday morning service. Watching from the back of the church, the new guy stood out. He made it obvious he was looking at me and really at first made me uncomfortable. After the church service we had a church Thanksgiving meal. I sat down to eat, and there he was. I said hi, asked who he was, where he came from. He said his name was Frank and that he was from Idaho, but then also said Washington State. He said he was a Nashville songwriter. I thought, *"This is so cool!* We have a songwriter here." He complimented my singing which led me to say, jokingly, that maybe he could write a song for me. Music is very important to me. My family started a gospel group when I was little, and I had been singing all my life. I had always wanted to sing an original song but did not know how to write one.

I didn't think anything else about that guy until one Wednesday night at church. He came through the food line and said he had written a song for me. I thought, *"Wow, how cool is that? He wrote one for me!"* I was flattered. I gave my email address to him so that he could send the song to me. He said I could get the band to learn it and sing it one Sunday. I thought, *"This is it; I get my own song to sing."* Word was already getting around church that he was a very successful businessman who was building a million-dollar home on one of the church member's property. He was in his forties and already retiring.

Frank emailed the song to me, and we started talking about music. I told him that I had always wanted to write a song about all the messes I had been through, and he said he was curious to hear about those. I told him that the story was too long, but he said he had all day to listen. LISTEN! Someone to listen! I poured my whole life out to him over emails; I told him everything. He fished for my current status and because I thought he was trustworthy I told him all about my marriage issues. Within hours, he found out I had money and marriage problems. He said that he was looking for a business partner for his luxury limo liner tour bus company and that he was stressed because his other partner had backed out a few months prior. He also said that there were other members of our church that were buying in, even told me a few names. He said that his company was on track to make 1.3 million dollars in 2017. He said that because of my background in business I would make a great fit. To make things even better, he offered me the position of regional sales manager; he said that an email with a job packet would follow from his company along with details.

At this time, Will could sense that something was not right. Here this stranger came in, wrote a song for his wife and even told her he wanted her in the band he was starting.

Frank said he was building a recording studio on the land he was purchasing. Will and I fought about this to the point that I told Will he could not stop me from being in a band. I was naïve, but Will knew something was off with this guy. Will knew our marriage was in the ditch, and here this guy was offering all this to me. Within a few days, Will and I were at each other. I was blinded big time and only thinking about freedom and myself.

Frank had already pumped me up to the point that I stood up to Will and said I wanted a divorce, that I was done. All the hurts and pain trapped inside for the last six years poured out but mostly in action. Nevertheless, I was bitter to the core, and it showed. Frank sent a message later saying, "Just shoot me now." The authorities had just called him saying that someone had stolen his bank account information and drained his company accounts. I told him that was crazy, and that it was a good thing that banks were insured. He said his accounts had been frozen until the investigation was finished. I did think that was odd that the bank wouldn't allow him access to his accounts. He finished by saying that this was really going to hurt his business, that there were things that need to be purchased for their upcoming tour season. He hinted and said if I was going to make my "buy-in" with the company this would be a good time.

Within three days, I was at the bank getting cash for Frank for my so-called "buy-in" with his company. While standing at the bank I sent a text asking him exactly how much he needed to get by until funds were again available. He asked me to hang on while he contacted someone to confirm the amount needed. The amount needed, he said, was $15,521. I met him at the football field to deliver the cash; he said his attorney would draw up the documents for my five-percent ownership in the company. He then said, "Now are you sure about this? This means it's a done deal, and we're partners now." It was exciting thinking I was a part of something so successful and big! It felt like I MATTERED enough that he would ask me to be a part.

I asked if he had found a local bank yet; he mumbled, "Yes, where is a Wells Fargo?" I looked online and saw that there was a branch twenty miles away. Frank went on his way and said his attorney would be in touch with me. Later, he called saying he was in Longview, which was odd to me, it was in the opposite direction of where the Wells Fargo branch was; that's as far as my thought about that went.

Two days later, Frank left to go back to Washington State to be home with his kids for Christmas. He said he would be back in a few weeks to close on the land he was buying. The name he was using "Frank" was part of his middle name, and I asked what his first name was. He laughed off my question and said his first name was embarrassing; he said he would tell me on the next Friday when he was on the road. I thought, *Is this a game to him, and is his name really so bad that he cannot tell me?* The thought of it was short-lived, and I just waited. HA! If I only had known then the reason for his delay! There were already so many red flags going up, but I was not paying attention.

I was intrigued and captivated by this very successful and famous man. The stories of his business dealings and his singing career were very impressive to me. I mean, who do you know who has written a song for a hit TV series? Yes, he told me he had written a song for the series, Sons of Anarchy, and was offered $300,000. He said he had songs on hold in Nashville by recording artists; I asked who those were. He said that they wouldn't tell him who just yet but probably Reba or Lady A.

He gave me everything I was hungry for, well, hungry for at that time in my life: singing opportunities, helping with my photography business by offering to build a studio, and of course now that great business deal. He also poured on the Bible and talked a lot about Jesus. He knew that is what I wanted, a man to pray and study the Word with me, to take the spiritual lead, and he sure poured it on thick. Be careful what you whine about to God, because He may just give it to you. The desires of my heart were being offered up to me on this platter, but what I saw was not what I ended up getting.

# CHAPTER 7

# Preyed Upon, While They Prayed

This chapter is by far the hardest for me to write. Every time I sit down to write it, my heart races and my stomach feels so sick. Because I knew in order to write this chapter, I had to go back into one of the darkest places in my life, embarrassing and shameful moments. I start to type a sentence and then pause to allow my nerves to settle.

Over the next three weeks (while he was gone to Washington State), Frank and I had hour-long phone conversations. I say conversations, but the only one talking was Frank. He told me about all his business success, his Nashville recording contract, and how he sang with stars. This made my life look very insignificant. He told me how he was taken advantage of by his best friend and how he took the fall for that friend's criminal activity because of his Christian material distribution failure. He gave stories with detailed times and dates; he had explanations down perfectly. He was so believable. He told me that is why he could not pay back all his investors because he lost his company when his friend cheated him. Every conversation we had was about his company.

Frank kept pushing me to file a quit-claim deed on my property before my divorce from Will was finalized. I did not know what that was, but he said his attorney told him that's what I needed so that I could get a line of credit on the equity in my house. Each time I told him that I had not heard anything from the bank, it was like his character flipped. He became angry but then quickly turned it around. He kept saying that he had debt from his previous company that needed to be paid, that it was his ex-partner's fault because that ex-partner had abandoned the company, leaving Frank with all the debt.

Yes, a pattern was showing, but I couldn't see that in the moment. It was always someone else's fault. Frank was so good he could have received an award for best actor. I believed everything he said. Why? Because I was infatuated and had thrown all common sense to the wind, it seemed. I had been careless before, but this was a new level of carelessness, even for me.

Will came by to drop Emma off about a week after he had moved out. He had found documents online about Frank that said Frank was not who he said he was. Will was trying to protect me but was very agitated toward me too. When I looked at the papers, I felt it was all a misunderstanding because Frank had talked to me already about it. BUT I did not say anything to Will about my knowledge of these things. After I talked with Will, my heart was racing and in panic because I needed to speak to Frank about this. I was scared because I had given him all that cash, so a part of me needed to be reassured. I left the house to call him and ask about the things that had been found online and apparently what he had done at another cowboy church in Waco, Texas. Of course, he had the perfect story, and I believed it. He had a way with words and was quick with his responses; I just brushed it off once again.

My mind was all over the place, along with my emotions, thinking of Will and my marriage, to this guy's background. I was not thinking clearly, only reacting in the moment. Once again, I was headed down a road my heart was screaming at me not to take. Like sin, once it is tasted it becomes deeply rooted inside. Satan knew my triggers and used Will's reactions toward me and the situation to push me further away and closer to evil. Crazy, isn't it? Longing for tranquility in my life resulted in the illusion that I would find it outside of God's will. This seemed to be my only way to cope, and it had become a very destructive pattern in my life. "Frank" had become the "out" from the long nights of crying myself to sleep and freedom from the chaos, or so I thought. If only I had known what was about to happen.

When I left the house to call Frank and talk about my conversation with Will, Frank just laughed because he thought it was funny. He had the perfect answers for all I had been told and all that was found on Google search. He even said "Good thing I told you the full story of what happened before now..." as if he knew he had already set me up. I chose to believe him, even though God was showing me proof that something was not right.

A few weeks later, my friend Jamie and I took our kids

to Great Wolf Lodge; I just needed to get away with my kids and have some fun. Life had been so stressful over the past years, and I wanted time with them. That night, I had messages from Will that were not pleasant. I also received a long text from a man I had gone to church with. His text was very judgmental and not sent in love, from what I could tell. From the words in that text, I thought my church was only hearing one side, and because my sin was so public, it was easy for people to believe that problems in my marriage were all my fault. That text hurt; I was done being hurt by people, especially men. As I read the words of disappointment from that text, it raised up more walls. I was also hurt because I really needed this time with my kids, and so many were ruining it! My thoughts at that time were, *I am trying to get away from the drama and chaos, and of course it has followed me everywhere I go.* I felt I was being manipulated from all ends; apparently I was an easy target for that.

I tried to enjoy the next three weeks with my kids, just relaxing and having fun with them. It was nice not to have to please any man at that point because in the end my kids were where my joy came from. Knowing there was nothing to worry about in those days, having fun, and not having any yelling or drama in our house, made me feel like I had taken chaos away from them. I was ever so blinded to the hidden hurt as the result of our family loss in them and even in myself. Selfishness and Satan are great deceivers.

**"The heart is deceitful above all things and beyond cure. Who can understand it?"
Jeremiah 17:9**

Frank did not say when he was coming back to Texas and

had now been gone for three weeks. When I finally asked him about it, he said, "Honestly, I'm out of money." I exclaimed, "WHAT? You have no money? And your company does not have money?" He said, "Yes, the company does have money. I did not save enough personal money because by now my partners should have been selling tickets for my company." I was very confused but apparently not enough to make me question him more in depth. He told me that because my money was not coming fast enough for my company buy-in it was hurting the company and the sale of tickets. Part of me did not understand that; how could it be my fault when before I ever really knew him he was saying his company was successful (remember his company on track to sell 1.3 million that year?) Common sense was being drowned out by manipulation and games.

I asked how much money he needed to return here; he said $3,000. I told him I could get $2,000. I told him I would deposit the money into the Wells Fargo account where he had previously deposited my buy-in money. I called the bank, and the lady I spoke with said they were just an office of the bank. Confused yet again, I asked, "So, I cannot deposit money there at all?" She said no, and that the closest one was three hours away. I called Frank and questioned him about the deposit he had made earlier with the money I had given him. I could tell he was scrambling for words. He said he would call back when he found out where he had made the deposit (Really, he can't remember?) I know, another red flag hitting me right upside the face. A few minutes later, he called and said he had deposited the money in Atlanta, Texas, which was almost three hours from where I had sent him to deposit the money. I still did not understand how he had driven three hours northeast in the opposite direction and never mentioned that he had, but again my common sense was drowned out.

I agreed to wire the money to him but was flagged when wiring it. I had to answer multiple questions to Western Union, "Have you ever met this man in person?" "How long have you known him?" "Have you spoken to him on the phone?" As I answered each question, my stomach climbed further and further up into my throat. Part of me thought, *"This is such a sign, Amy! You're waiting for the agent to save you from yourself."* I had allowed manipulation to infect my every move, and like my past behavior I just went wherever I was led.

Frank was headed back to Texas, and he started asking me about a business office to rent for his company and RV parks where he could stay in his RV. I found one, but he left it open for me to call and pay, I knew he had no "personal" money, so it was left for me to foot the bill. He promised to repay the previous money along with the money I paid for his office space. The business side of me that Daddy instilled said, "Do not spend money if you do not have it." I did not understand Frank's outlook on this. He was so smooth with words and told me this was what had to be done. He even asked if I knew of anyone that could make sales calls for him. *Well, no, because I had no one in my life anymore.* Plus, I knew that he had no money to pay anyone. Moreover, deep inside I was embarrassed about our relationship and his so-called business.

Frank kept wanting me to quit my radio job because he said I could make more money with him. I did not see any money coming in; I knew my divorce would soon be final, and I needed my job. He began to ask me things like "When will the divorce be final," and I would give him a date. He would ask, "Is that when you get the money out," but I told him I did not know. I called the bank but I could tell this was not going to be something easy; it was going to take longer than was expected. I was not in as much as a rush as he was. I guess he tried to be in control of just how pushy he was so as not to set off any red flags.

When I found out that the money would not be there on the divorce date and told Frank, he became outraged. He told me that "….all these stupid bankers can't get their stuff right;" I told him this was the process. He told me that he'd told the people he owed money to that they would have their money on that day. I suggested that maybe he didn't need to make a promise until he had money in hand. All the while I felt like I was good for nothing except money. This inheritance had been nothing but trouble for the past eight years. It seemed that money was pure evil. Even if I had not used it for myself in selfish ways, it seemed it always brought out evil in others around me; I had used it as a cushion to escape my problems.

Frank had my credit cards and was using them. He told me that he needed to buy two tickets from his website because it would look good to show some sales. He used my credit card and bought over $7,000 worth, and that money went into his bank account. I asked him a few days later when that money would be given back so that I could pay my credit card account. He quickly responded, "Yeah, going to work on that." He kept saying he was going to pay me back next month for the other purchases. He said that it was the lady's fault that had backed out of the buy-in last year that had put him in this bind, and now it was this holdup with my money.

At the end, anything I felt or said, he would put me in my place; I felt like I was just to be seen and not heard. I began to see that my opinion was not welcome at all. I tried to please him and make him see me as worthy. Pretty sad writing that, knowing that is how I felt. He began to have anger issues with me. I was so tired of hearing about the company. Every day something changed. He called his lawyer who said that he would be his partner. Every day it seemed there was a new partner, a new goal, always changing the names and numbers on his spreadsheets. It was all getting to the point where I was not listening anymore, and he saw that.

When Frank did not have my attention, he would explode. I had been yelled at in times prior to this, but this was a whole new level. His brown eyes would turn black. He would become so mad that he spit with each word that came out of his mouth. I would cower down in my chair. I was again trapped in abuse. I would just sit there and take it because, well, that's how I saw myself, worthless, unworthy of anything else. I had no clue just how bad it was going to become.

Two weeks passed, and I questioned him about money because he had been buying things. He told me that the money was from ticket sales coming through. I was sick thinking of how he was using ticket money for his own personal use. When I questioned him, he told me that's how he gets paid and that he didn't take a paycheck for all his work. My mind was racing, *"This isn't good business practice."* I was caught up in my own personal emotions with kids, Will, the divorce and now this. There was so much that I just did not question anymore because I knew his answers didn't make sense.

On Valentine's night we went to eat. Frank paid with his business bank card, which made me wonder whose money he was using. I felt dirty already and even more so knowing that he paid with money from who-knows-where. When I dropped him back to his office, as soon as he got to the door the deputy yelled his name. I watched in shock as he was handcuffed. Frank told me to call his lawyer; I shook as he gave me the number. I asked the Deputy why Frank was being taken into custody, and he gave me two pieces of paper..FRAUD! Frank told me it was not true and even went as far as to say it was because of the language barrier. "Language barrier?" What, Texan versus Yankee? He said that the people he was trying to help buy into the company from my church had misunderstood him and what he was saying. In my mind somewhere, I promise, that made no sense either. I had already drunk the Kool-Aid at that point because I had been "talked at" for weeks, all day-every day, leading up to that moment.

As Frank was handcuffed and put into the back of the deputy's car, he said he had been set up because we were together. He even told the deputy it was Will's fault. This was all so much. I was standing there while my two older kids were in my car on the other side of his truck. I hoped they did not see too much. I did not know what to think as

I was trying to process what was happening.

Frank called me later that night from jail, cool as a cucumber. I thought, *"Does he not understand what is going on?"* He had been arrested for two counts of fraud. He told me it was all because of me and him. He insisted he did not do anything wrong, that he had the right to sell part of his company without a license. His lawyer even called me from up North and told me the same thing, that this was all a witch hunt, that Will and his law enforcement friends were all behind it. He also told me he needed $15,000. for bail.

The next day I went to his office to get my laptop Frank had been using. As I opened it, all his email accounts were still open and logged into. I read one, then another and another. After reading the last one, I could hardly catch my breath. There were emails from old customers that he owed money to who were threatening to get the law involved if he did not pay. He always responded to them with a lie, that he had been out of range or sick in the hospital. I went back twelve months in the email accounts, and they were all lies.

That night I began hunting down some people in his life; I had not spoken to anyone Frank knew this whole time I had known him. I found a lady that was on the company bank account and who was a part of his company. She acted shocked and even gave me the bank information so I could see if there was money there. I got online and pulled up the records. SHOCKED! No money. What I discovered was that the tickets bought with my credit card had gone into the account, and he was using that money to live off of. He also had never deposited any of the cash I had given him. I added up over $1,000. in overdraft fees; he had used the card knowing and not caring that there were overdraft fees.

I went back to the date that the account was opened; $250,000. was deposited into the account and was depleted within six months. The lady that I had called who was listed as president of the company told me that $200,000. was her buy-in to this "thriving" company. Her husband had given $50,000. for his buy-in. She could not believe that Frank was a bad guy. I was just trying to find out the truth.

Frank called and I questioned him about the money I had given to him; he said that it all went to company stuff. He blamed the lack of growth on this lady and her husband for not selling tickets; he said that they could not complain because they were supposed to be working. He had something good in response to every question I asked. I could not explain my behavior. It was as if common sense was telling me he was up to no good, but then the other part of me that apparently was at the helm was in denial BIG time.

The day after his arrest was mine and Will's divorce court date. I was so sad, mad and hurt all at once with everything. At that moment we stood up in front of the judge, I thought, *"Is he just going to let me go just like that?"* I thought he would tell the judge to stop this because, duh, I had basically lost my mind, but just like that it was over. I think back and wonder how easy it seemed to be for the judge to sign away a marriage, a family split up and kids torn apart. But then it was over, and here laid at my feet was a man in jail. I had no job, and everything I had been told looked like a lie. I thought I was indebted to Frank, though for what I was not sure. He had convinced me that I was the cause of this and that he had left his kids and home for me.

WAIT a second, what? Frank had told others before he had even met me that he was moving here to Texas, was going to build this huge house and recording studio. I knew this was not true, and YET I acted and responded as if it were. Yes see, at this point I was not controlling anything from within the depths of who I was. I had made some quick mistakes from emotions before, yes, but deep in my core this was completely going against what I knew to be true. This was a first. I had become further and further away from my truth.

Money. I had always been good with money. NO debt other than a home loan. Now I was sitting here allowing my good credit and cash go into this never-ending hole that was Frank. At this point, all the games, lies, manipulation and verbal abuse had worked their magic. I was just a girl, stuck in the shadow of an abusive criminal. He knew how to get to me. When I reached out to others in his past, their stories seemed off, but he would call and have a story ready to counteract theirs. He even had the nerve to tell me to go ahead with the loan. I saw then that I was just a cash cow, a means to an end. There were moments I stopped and tried to feel once again, but the hurt shut those feelings down. This pain, where was all this pain coming from? I did not want to feel, so I shut off all the feelings just like that. Why was it that I would rather walk right off a cliff than face my pain?

## CHAPTER 8

# How Could It Get Any Worse? Just Give Me Enough Rope.

Frank's bail was set at $15,000. and he was unable to pay. I was still walking around in a daze from all that had gone on. Arrested, but why? I was so confused. He called me from jail in a very weakened state, giving me names and numbers of some past customers to ask them if they would loan him the money for bail. I was very uncomfortable doing this, so his lawyer handled it. I was back and forth with my feelings and thoughts.

Looking for some answers, I reached out through Facebook to an ex-girlfriend/partner in Frank's company. What I was told was that Frank was a con man and a narcissist with twenty-five years of scamming under his belt. This lady said the best place for him was in jail so that he could not hurt anyone else. The story Frank told me sounded like someone that had just had a lot of bad luck and was misunderstood. He was still trying to repay past investors, or so he made it seem. I was only seeing this situation on the surface, and there was so much more than the eye could see. Crushed from my divorce and suffocating in my past, I was not strong enough to dig deeper into the truth of the man Frank truly was. I started thinking, *"Maybe he's not a good man, what have I gotten myself into?"* I had given him money and was working on giving him even more. I confronted him about things over the phone while he was in jail, and he again had these stories that made sense.

I chose to go see the local county investigator that was working on Frank's case. This investigator told me that Frank was the best manipulator he had ever seen in his forty years of work. He told me he understood how I could fall for it, but he was in fact a scammer. He explained that Frank had been to other churches in Texas trying to do the same thing he had done here. Frank had broken off a relationship with a pastor from another church right before he walked into my church. I sat there, tears in my eyes, trying my best not to blink because if I did blink the investigator would see that I was crying. Crying for what? The thought that it could be true, plus he had already taken over $15,000. cash from me and run up my credit cards? The investigator said, "Good thing he didn't get anything from you." As he said that, I said in a muffled tone, "I gave him money," and in that moment I was embarrassed. As I continued to listen to the description from the investigator, this did not sound like the guy I had spent hours with me on the phone, listening to his life and how misunderstood he was by others. Was I really another victim?

When Frank called later that evening, I confronted him about all I had been told. He again had the best answers;

I was not sure who to believe. The next day I went to visit him in jail. This was a first. I walked into a room with these little stools and a big glass window. He walked out and sat down; he appeared to be humbled in that moment. I was numb at that point, no tears, nothing. I just sat there looking at him in his orange jumpsuit. I sat there thinking, *"This has become my life. I'm sitting in a jail talking to… Who is he? Who am I?"*

Along with the many that had begun calling me to talk about Frank, an agent from the State of Texas called. He asked me to come to Dallas for an interview. I remember thinking, *"How do I go from a normal life to now being interviewed by the State Securities Agency?"* I drove to Dallas and was interviewed and recorded. I told them everything, and the agent knew all about me. My thought was, *"How does he know about my most personal dealings?"* He sounded more like a therapist than an investigator. I was in tears the whole time. I told him about the money I had already invested and the credit card use by Frank. He asked so many questions; most I had no answer for because I did not know at all, really. I knew nothing of Frank's life. I only knew of the hour-long stories he would tell, which were very detailed ones.

As I sat across from the agent, my phone constantly vibrated on the table. I told him that it was Frank calling. I became more and more nervous each time the phone went off. As I was leaving Dallas, Frank called again, and I answered. "I've made bail," he said, and my heart fell right into my gut. *"What do I do?"* A part of me wanted to run, a part of me felt I should fix it, and a part of me wished I could grow a backbone and be all right telling him to go to you-know-where. I had been told years earlier that I needed someone to teach assertiveness lessons to me so that I wouldn't get run over anymore. Maybe if I had listened I could have stood up to a lot of these men, but I never wanted to be one of those women, either.

Some of Frank's past customers wired money to me into my account. This made me extremely nervous, and then I said I couldn't be involved. I was going to send it back to them and tell them to find another way to bail him out. Frank called and I told him I could not be involved, and he became very upset. I could hear the gritting of his teeth as he was trying to control his anger. He told me he had given up his bed to an older man, that he had nowhere to sleep and how could I just leave him in there. I hung up the phone only to have it ring again. It was his daughter pleading with me to go and get him. Again, I heard how he was a really good guy and just misunderstood. I finally gave in.

Later that evening I went to meet a bail bondsman; I had no clue about that process. I did not know how bail/bonding worked. I sat in the bondsman's office watching him prepare the paperwork with my stomach in knots. I was in tears pretty much the whole time. We walked over to the jail, and I sat and waited. By this time, word had already gotten out that I was getting Frank out of jail. Will sent a text too, "Amy, what are you doing?" My phone kept going off with text after text. The door opened; Frank was free. I looked at him and thought, *What am I doing? This is crazy, Amy!*

After only two days of his being out of jail, I was completely sucked into Frank's charms. Daily he would say, "Oh Amy, you are my everything, I need you…." He promised a life that I really did not believe because deep inside I knew he was not who he said he was. I now understand why people kidnap their loved ones from cults and take them somewhere private to detox them because they have literally been brainwashed.

I was worried about his legal issues but he acted like they weren't anything. He said that he had received no money from anyone, so they couldn't find him guilty of any charges. I became very nervous as I began to tell him about my trip to Dallas and the recorded interview with the investigator. He grew quite upset, and I saw in his face and eyes that he was ready to let me have it. He said, "How could you do this to me?" He then asked if I had told the investigator about the money I had given to him. I told him that I had told them everything. Frank told me that I should have stayed out of his business. I spoke up and asked him, "What was I supposed to think? You had been arrested. Investigators were not asking but telling me to come in to be interviewed." I was not about to lie, and I had been sworn in before the interview. He really laid a guilt trip on me then because of this....so much so that I agreed to marry him, mostly because in some twisted way I felt I had wronged him. He was good at manipulating every situation to his advantage. If he and I were married, maybe it wouldn't look bad that he had sold me securities for his company, plus wives don't have to testify against their husbands.

Off we headed to Arkansas just two weeks after my divorce from Will. I don't even have words to explain my actions because there are none. We were married and then headed right back home. The next day I was scared, *"What in the world did I just do? Amy, No! You've really done a doozy this time.*" I did not want to tell anyone, not even my kids. I tried to convince Frank that he could just stay in his camper like he had been doing and not move into the house. No one would ever know. He was insulted by that arrangement. I had to tell my kids, and that was the hardest thing I had ever done. I knew they did not like it, even though they would not ever say it to me. I was so disappointed in myself, so I knew they would be as well. Nonetheless, I regretted this and tried to secretly contact the man who would be turning in the marriage license the following Tuesday.

After we got married, I stopped pursuing the loan and stopped calling to check on it because of all the uncertainty. Frank confronted me about my lack of interest in getting the loan. I told him I just couldn't go through with it because I felt this wasn't what God would want me to do, to put myself and my kids in this financial burden. He stood up from the chair, came over to where I was and slammed my laptop down, all the while cussing and yelling at me. He said that I was pulling a "bait and switch." I didn't know what "bait and switch" was, but I knew it must mean that I had changed my mind. He told me that I had better not dare start bringing God into this, that I had made a business deal with him and I needed to stick to something for once in my life. (he was always ready to throw up my past to further his gain).

When Frank exploded like that I would make some excuse to leave and would text and call a friend. A few times I met up with Will to talk. Each time I talked to him, I'm sure he was hopeful I would finally leave Frank. Will said if I wanted he would contest our divorce, which would make my and Frank's marriage invalid. But it seemed that no one was willing to do something radical to stop the bleeding. I felt I was left with making the best of my self-induced situation.

Watching how Frank was running his so-called business, however, was a hard pill to swallow. Throughout all of this, I was still sneaking texts and calls to my friend and to Will. I had moments of resolve but would end up frozen in fear, would get nervous and shut everyone out again.

One day I told Frank I had a photoshoot. At this point, my photoshoot money was buying our food; he never questioned me about leaving for those shoots. I went to my friend's house, ready to talk. I needed to pour everything out. I needed someone to listen, and I wanted to talk. In their rush to free me from Frank, they wanted to go to my house and get him out. We went to my house to tell him to leave; I was a crying mess all the way there and was not in any condition to stand up against someone like him. I went inside the house; Frank did not know that three of my friends and two of their husbands were outside. They all said they would give me five minutes, and then they were coming in. As I went inside, I found Frank putting his shoes on; he saw the look on my face as I stood there. He said, "What's wrong?" I replied, "I can't do this anymore. This has gotten way over my head with you and all your business dealings."

Frank grinned and said he was not going anywhere. I felt sick. My joints locked up, and I could not move my body towards the door. The next thing I heard was my friends coming into my house and into the room where we were. They told him to get out and that I wanted him gone. He locked the door and would not leave, so I said I'd leave. I grabbed my bag and started making my way to leave. He took my keys and locked me out of the bedroom. I went outside and waited with my friends. As I sat in the hammock on my porch, my friends tried in their own way, to take back some part of my life; I could not even fight for myself.

My friend, Jamie, and I sat there talking. She was the calm one, so it gave me a little peace as the others were in the house trying to get Frank to leave. My friends were pure warrior chicks, and they were there to literally fight for me. But nothing that they said was working; he would not leave. He came out and gave me the stare down and wanted to talk to me alone. Everyone told me not to go back in there alone with him. He told me I was going to regret this and made me feel like I was walking away from a good thing. No matter what I said, he was not going to leave! I didn't do much talking because I didn't know what to say in the moment; I was so brain dead. My thoughts really were on lockdown.

At this point my friends did all the talking for me and even called the cops. The Marshall arrived and said that he could not get Frank to leave the house because he lived there. I left with my friend, Jamie, and went to her house for a while; the whole time I was there my phone was going off. Frank had his partner text me to say that Frank was suicidal and that she was worried about him. I became worried, so on my way to spend the night at my other friend's house I stopped to check on him. He had been placed on suicide watch when he was arrested, so I was concerned that he might try to do something. Why did I care? I still was so confused. What I should have been thinking was about me and my kids and that is all. I could not get him out of my head. He had worked too long and too hard at being in there full time. When I arrived at the house, I had been locked out. I went to the back door, knocked just to see if he was all right, then I would leave, or at least that was my plan. He opened the door and I was told to get in the house. I knew then it was a mistake coming back.

Frank grabbed my keys and would not let me leave. I had to endure hours of him screaming and yelling the worst things anyone could be called. He degraded me and my family. He called my friends the worst possible names, blamed me for his arrest and the lack of growing his business. He told me I was disgusting and that looking at me made him sick. I was so overcome with fear; my legs were shaking as I was trying to get away from his presence. I was truly afraid, *"God, please keep me safe, please!"*

As I tried to get past him, he grabbed my arms and told me I was not going anywhere. I sat down at the dining room table, and he kept on with his tirade. He did not even take a breath. He said, "How dare you try to have me removed from MY home!" He then went for my weak spot, me as a mother. He knew that would shut me down emotionally because he knew I was hardest on myself in that area. I just broke.

I began to apologize and told him he was right. How sad I am for the woman I was at that moment. But I was BROKEN. I felt trapped like a caged animal. I knew my thoughts and weaknesses would keep me imprisoned to him. He told me to immediately delete my friends' numbers from my phone and to never speak to them again. I was trying to sneak a text to one of them to let her know that I wouldn't be coming so she would know what had happened, but I couldn't. I was able to write out a text that he approved and sent to the other friend.

For the next few weeks I dove into the Word; that's all I had left. "God, forgive me for spitting in Your face, complaining about where You had me in my previous marriage. Please God, forgive me," I prayed aloud as I sat in my hammock. I knew I had lost it all. Yes, my previous marriage had been a mess, but I had blown the chance to even watch, wait and see how God could restore it because I was selfish. My family was broken, and I had not seen my step-daughter whom I missed so much. How had I allowed this to happen? I stayed in my Bible and in prayer for weeks; day by day, I grew stronger. Frank saw that and even insulted me and criticized me for being outside alone for so long. The more I was away from him and the more I was in the Bible and in prayer, something inside of me began to take root. God had not left me. He was waiting there all along…I went to Him humbled and repentant. I was broken, but I felt I was becoming stronger. He was preparing me for freedom. I could finally taste that freedom, believing that I could do this and that I could, in fact, get away from Frank.

Frank had planned to go to Nashville to record his songs. He had asked me a month prior to send a guy a $1,000. deposit to hold his recording spot. At that point, I had very little money left. I asked him how he was going to come up with the other $5,000. He said "Let me worry about that." I sent the deposit, and a recording date was set. A few days before he was going to leave, I asked about the other money that was due; he said he was waiting on it. If I remember this correctly, Becky, a travel agent from Texas, was selling tickets for a tour to Mount Rushmore; she would then deposit the money into his company's account. I had a sick feeling in my gut, a well-earned sick feeling.

Later, I went to Frank and said, "I just cannot be a part of this, knowing you are using customers' ticket money for your recordings." He became so upset and scolded me, saying "How dare you come in here and tell me that! You are inconsiderate and selfish!" He ended up going anyway; I could only afford to pay $50. per night for a motel. He complained about that afterwards; he said hopefully someone he had reached out to would give him money. I believe that he had emailed a guy named Stephen and another old investor named Tom. *I just did not understand how he was headed to Nashville to record without money. This is not sane behavior,"* I thought. He literally was waiting for money to fall from the sky.

When he left, I had a breakdown and wished that I was strong enough to have gotten him out of the house. It would've been easy since he was gone for two days. He came back from that trip in a very bad mood, ignoring me and going right to bed. The next day he told me how selfish I had been, how I only thought of myself. He said that he was the one that had to be humiliated at the recording (which I never asked about so not sure what was said) and slept in a nasty motel. He also gave me a guilt trip because I wouldn't pay the recording producer the rest of the money with my PayPal credit card. I had, for five months, up until then paid for all his living expenses and then some. I stood there thinking, *"Selfish?"* I knew I had to figure a way out, but I was still struggling emotionally. It was hard because he made me feel like I was the problem. He told me I needed to get help and that I was crazy. Yes, I was crazy! How on earth did I allow this parasite into my life unless I had gone cuckoo?

I began to see more and more lies, and Frank didn't even try to hide them at this point. I even heard him pretending to be a man named Jasper when calling travel agents. Yes, he could sell it; he was very charming and persuasive with his clients. He had his business model and used some of my money to create and purchase beautiful brochures for luxury, all-inclusive seven-day limo-liner bus tours with a personal chef, personal tour guide, the whole nine yards. I watched it all unfold; everything that I was warned about was happening. There was no money and no limo-liner, yet he was taking elderly, retired people's money and spending every dime on himself and his past debts, or I should say the debts that were the most threatening and who had said they would get the law involved if not paid. At this point, he had drained all the equity in my house and run up all my credit cards, so he was desperate for ticket sales. I became nauseated watching this happen.

I told Frank I did not want to lose my home, and his response was "I've lost my mine before, and it's not the end of the world." He scolded me for questioning things and told me, "We're married now, Amy; this is my house and my money, too." I was taken back by his arrogance. This was just one of the many things that added to the pile of panic screaming, *"Get out Amy! You're fixing to be homeless!"*

He had asked for my social security number, and I refused to give that to him. I knew that I couldn't let that fall into his hands. I needed to research his past on my own so that I could understand it and not just go by what others were saying. The only time I could do that was when he would sleep. I would sneak and look at his laptop, phone and boxes of papers he had stored away. With each email, text and paper I read, my heart became more panicked, but with that came clarity of who this guy really was. I thought, *"Who keeps all the incriminating evidence of themselves?"*

I saw from afar that Will was going on with his life. This made me mad and sad all at the same time. Why could he not have put in the work on our marriage before I left again? He was going to come later to get Emma but sent his daughter instead. I had not seen her in a few months. As she drove up, I lost it, tears flowing as I hugged her so tightly and did not want to let go. I said to her over and over, "I'm so sorry, please forgive me." I looked over and saw she had other people in the car, and they, too, saw my breakdown. I knew then I had to get my life in order so I could be a part of her life in some way, even if just as a friend.

When she left, my sadness turned into anger. I sent Will a text message asking how he could do this to me. It was like rubbing salt into an open wound, having the embarrassment of my meltdown with his daughter in front of the other girls that were with her. All at once, pain and hurt came over me. Most of the pain surfaced from our first four years of marriage. I thought of how I never once told anyone about what he was doing behind closed doors, never made it public. However, it was like, as soon as Amy messed up, he would tell everyone. I was angry and broken-hearted all at once. I flooded his phone with it all, and he ignored me. I told myself that his silence was confirmation that *"See, I really am worth nothing."*

# CHAPTER 9
# The Hard Step Back

Monday June 5, 2017 - I was pacing around the house that day. My chest was tight, and I felt every heartbeat pound throughout my whole body. I walked into the bathroom, and to my surprise sometime earlier that morning my daughter had written on the mirror, **"Trust in God, Jesus is love, never, ever, ever give up, you are my sunshine, love you Momma, stay true to yourself, believe in yourself."** She didn't have a clue that God was working through her with each word; to this day those words remain on my mirror, untouched.

My mom had texted me asking to take the kids to the movies; Wonder Woman of all things. I told Frank, and his response was, "You take them there, drop them off and do not talk to your mom." Over the next few hours, my mom changed her mind and decided to take them the next day instead. I knew I had to find a way out, but how? I felt trapped. Frank was leaving the following week to head to his daughter's graduation in Washington State, and I knew that would be the time for me to rid him from my life. I started planning, but God showed me that day that He had it planned differently.

Up to this point, I felt like the elephant that had its spirit broken. (Google that; it's a very sad process.) None of my thoughts were mine anymore. Every thought and action had been centered around Frank and what he wanted from me. I had an acquaintance named Stephanie who came to mind, but I quickly dismissed that thought. I did not want her to think I was using her because my other friends had become so upset with me after I went back to Frank this last time. I stared at my phone with this presence surrounding me – *Do it, Amy NOW!* It was like I was in a pressure cooker with the temperature rising minute by minute. I felt that if I did not do something fast my heart would beat right out of my chest. I had to be sneaky so Frank would not find out I was calling her, so I lied and said I was going to be on the phone with the credit card company. He was busy doing something, so after staring at my phone laying there on my bed, I knew it was now or never. I grabbed my phone and messaged Stephanie to call me right then. The phone rang. I locked the door to my room and told her everything right down to every dirty secret I ever had.

After I was finished talking, she said she had been praying the whole time I was talking to her. She said that she had some things that she felt like the Lord wanted her to say. What poured out of her mouth for the next five minutes were words anointed by the Holy Spirit - words that were just normal words but had heavenly power behind them.

It was as if doors and windows had opened, and the power from the heavens surrounded me. She reminded me of who I was in Christ; I am His. She told me that others might think I am sick, but she said that I was not sick, that I was broken and had a lot of trauma that needed to be healed. She said that all the much-needed healing I longed for and craved I would pour into others. I was so thirsty and desperate for healing myself; I was dried up and so thirsty that I drank whatever was available. Everything she said made complete sense. She called Frank out for who he was…the devil in disguise. He was pure evil and the fruit of my sin, and our so-called marriage was a product of that sin. She then prayed over me with power and strength in the Name of Jesus.

I got down on my knees and curled up on the floor with the phone close to my ear as I felt that power pour into my very core. I can't explain how I felt in words because it was not of this earth. It was heaven sent to my body. Stephanie told me to rise, stand firm and if I didn't know what to say to keep repeating the Name of Jesus. I got up with the power of the Holy Spirit running through my body. I had strength and courage in me that was ready for war. With that one step of faith, I had to make it on my own. It was the scariest, most frightful thing I had ever done. As much as I wanted to be with God, I felt the demonic power pulling me back. It was a battle. I told God, "I have nothing left, but I trust You with the little crumb I do have."

That first step in obedience was all it took for the powers of Heaven to pour out and prepare my path. I was focused. I told Frank that I was taking the girls to my Mom's for the movie, and while he was not looking I grabbed a bag with a few of my personal things, knowing I would not be back until he was gone. I grabbed my girls and left, speaking the Name of Jesus softly on my lips. As I drove away in that strength, I felt the weight of hell lifted from me. I went to Will's house and waited. My girls were confused, as I had told them we were going to Nana's but had ended up at Will's. I just didn't know how to explain to them what I had just done; they wouldn't understand. I did not know what my next step would be, but I knew God had it and I was going to follow His lead.

Will had already moved on, or so I thought. Nowhere in my mind was the thought of us getting back together. Will had been fighting for my safety this whole time, and Stephanie knew I would be safe there. All this time he had tried to protect me from this evil I had allowed into my life. As I waited for Will to get home, I was nervous yet peaceful about what I had just done. Will arrived, and as we talked about my situation, I received a message from Frank asking about supper. He said, "Well I guess this means you are not going to back in time to cook supper." He had become very demanding with things, and meals was one of those things. I had to have supper ready at a certain time each day; I had become a servant to him. Gosh, that makes me sick, thinking of how I allowed him to get into my head like that and the control I allowed him to have over me. I replied to him something like I wanted him out of my house and that I was only worried about my emotional health and my kids. I was not in a place to be harsh to him, because what good would that do? I was only focused on making sure he got it into his head that this was the last message and contact he would get from me personally, and that one message was it.

I never spoke to him again.

Later, I was confronted by someone about all my choices. As I was listening to what they were saying I could not explain the peace I had at that very moment. They said I could lose my children, assuming I needed to be medicated (nothing like hearing that you're crazy!). In the past, this would have sent me into a hole. Now, I had peace because I was doing this crazy new thing called "trusting fully in God." The peace washed over me like warm water as the words being spoken to me bounced right off, as if God had placed a bulletproof vest over my heart, protecting me from the arrow. In the human eye, I did not deserve protection, yet His grace was abundant, and I settled into that. *Wow! God, after all my wrongs, you give me this?* It was amazing to be in His presence.

I had lost it all. All the money was gone. I was in major debt. My children had been taken for the moment, and I only had the clothes on my back. Yet, I felt I had everything! Now, that is something only God could do in the absolute mess I was in. I was faced with nothing but truth because I was stripped down to the rawness that I had never felt inside me before. No more control, no more self and no more trying. I had nothing left to give or for anyone to take. I felt His love in that dirtiest of moments more than what I thought were the cleanest moments of my life. How could it be, that with nothing I felt love, grace and the treasure in Him. In that moment I was determined to do whatever I had to do to heal. No more masking but true healing.

The next day I Googled "Christian counselors" and everyone in my area was booked for a month. I was crushed, thinking I had to navigate the next thirty days without any professional help. *I need one NOW, God!*" I sent a text to Will to let him know about the wait; he had graciously offered to pay all of my counseling costs. A few hours later, he called and said something weird had just happened. A friend of his walked into his office, and as they were talking Will asked his friend what his wife did. His friend responded that she was a counselor! Will responded, "Christian?" "Yes," his friend said, and her office was right here in Carthage. Will asked me if that was too close to home and if I would be comfortable pouring out my life and all my issues to her. I said, "I DO NOT CARE! I have NO pride left!" When someone is ready for real change, they do not have time to be picky. I called this counselor, but she could not see me until the following week. That was better than not being able to see someone for a month. Ten minutes later, and the counselor called back to say there had been a cancellation for the next day. I was like, *"God. You've got this, don't you? Thank You for not making me wait days."*

The first session was hard. I knew this counselor outside her practice and was anxiously awaiting in embarrassment to unload all of my ugliness. She said, "All right, how I usually start off is by asking where you are today, what's going on that brought you here to me, and then we will work backward from there." I was thinking, *"She's fixing to get an earful!."* I did not waste any time and blurted out, "I divorced my husband and married a con artist." Her eyes became big and she said, "Wait, back up, you and Will got a divorce?" Then she said, "Let's start from the beginning, then we will move forward."

With each word, each divorce and each marriage I felt so ashamed of myself. I thought, "*She probably thinks I am one of those crazy ladies from a Lifetime movie. That is why I did not go back after that one counseling session after Emma's birth. That is why I faked I am all right, now.*" This was some painful stuff; my stomach was in knots and my palms were sweaty. I had not even made it through all my marriages when the time was up; she quickly said "strongholds." She then challenged me to get real with my past and said that in the next session we would dig deeper.

The next session the counselor knew something was not right when I talked about my childhood, "my daddy this, my daddy that." She could sense something was off by how perfectly I painted my childhood, sitting here on her sofa, lying through my teeth. She challenged me, and I told her, "No ma'am, my childhood was the greatest."

She said, "Amy, go back to that little girl."

I was thinking, "*No, I cannot go there. Not there. I love my daddy too much.*"

I kept avoiding it, and she kept going deeper and deeper into more details. In a meek voice I said, "Well there was some fighting and there was yelling…" as I said those words to her out came some flashbacks to those moments in that instant, heartache flooded my soul. "No, it does not have to be said because it did not affect me!"

She said, "Amy, more than you know, it has."

With my body trembling and my skin already broken out in hives (apparently I do this quite often) I shouted in a broken, hysterical voice, "The same man who I have placed on a pedestal is the same man who abused us?"

I felt like I was a balloon that had been deflated. There was no air left in my lungs because it took every bit of that air to speak those words. I sat there and cried; I felt badly that I had even said it. "I am so sorry, Daddy," I said with tears flowing down my face. I was thinking, "Oh no, now someone knows." I had NEVER told anyone. I had been my daddy's biggest cheerleader; in that moment, with a few words I had just thrown him under the bus. In my eyes, my daddy was and always will be a great man. I never held anything against him, so why would I feel the need to tell or speak of those things to anyone? What I did not know was that all the abuse had carved away at my self-image and worth and wired my mind to react to would-be triggers throughout my life. I never knew that.

There was a hidden secret monster alive in my head, moving and rearranging my actions to each situation. It was all beginning to make sense to me; real and raw these thoughts hurt to the touch. As each session took place, I began to dig deeper, and it's no wonder I behaved and reacted this way. It was becoming the biggest breakthrough of my life! It was as if I was working out the puzzle of my life. There were missing pieces, and as I found each one I placed it in its place to see the picture become clearer and clearer.

I found that learning and finding confidence, knowing that I had a voice, that I could say no, and knowing what my feelings were and that they are relevant was empowering. My perceptions were valid. I could not get enough of this new freedom in "talking." I poured myself into counseling weekly. I even went to a psychologist and had a test performed that took about four hours. The results of the test were amazing. It is crazy how with all the questions they asked from blocks and drawings they found out how I am wired. It was even more empowering that I could renew my mind just as the scriptures said, that with the way I was thinking and with the struggles I had, I could find rest.

## A PORTION OF MY TEST RESULTS

*She has a significant dependent personality trait. Individuals with these types of profiles tend to be easily led by others and lean on others for security, support, guidance and direction. They are often easily manipulated and exploited. They often tend to willingly submit to the wishes of others in order to maintain a sense of security in their lives. She may engage in a lot of self-defeating behaviors and thinking patterns. Appears to be anxious, intense and has difficulty concentrating or making routine decisions. Struggles with worry, guilt and depression. She is apparently highly distressed, though this may be a situational component in her life. She may have some panic symptoms as well. Experiencing generalized fears. Tendency to be insecure and nonassertive in social situations and generally tends to be prone to guilt feelings, ruminating excessively about personal and interpersonal failings. She may have perfectionistic standards as well. She is introverted and has difficulties meeting other people.*

By including some of my test results, I'm hoping that they will give you some kind of knowledge as to why I may have responded and reacted to certain situations, as well as some understanding as to why we do things that we really do not want to do. There are root issues behind all of our destructive behaviors. I did not understand why I reacted the way I did for so long, the panic, the tight chest, the running away from loud noises, the pressure to get home and the meltdowns while doing the simplest of things. I thought it was just me, how I was made up and how my brain had been wired all those years ago. It was the greatest eye-opening experience I had ever had. It was not easy; it was a very painful emotional process that I refused to give up on.

I have watched God transform the insecurities I struggled with for years. It was not this overnight-Cinderella moment. It was a day-by-day commitment to the process, and each day turned into weeks and months. I was living out God's truth, even though it was at times harder on me than childbirth! He calls us to meditate on what is "pure," and now I know why. Destructive patterns keep us responding to situations in our lives with destructive behaviors.

**"Whatsoever things are TRUE, whatsoever things are HONEST, whatsoever things are JUST, whatsoever things are PURE, whatsoever things are LOVELY, whatsoever things are of GOOD REPORT; if there is any VIRTUE, and if there be any PRAISE, think on these things." - Philippians 4:8**

I was beginning my new journey of healing, but I was still married to Frank and had to get that resolved. I again had NO money to my name for the legal work. Will's lawyer knew of the mess I was in. He was there throughout the whole thing when Will tried to fight for our marriage. Knowing that, the attorney did all the paperwork for my divorce from Frank at no charge. He informed me that my marriage to Frank was not even legal because in Texas there was a thirty-day waiting period from the time a divorce is final. At that time I was focused on two things: my personal mental health and healing and removing Frank from my life both legally and mentally.

# CHAPTER 10

# The End Started My New Beginning

As I sit here completing the ending of this book of the life I lived for the first thirty-seven years, I still cannot believe that it is my story to tell. I could do the whole "what if" game – what if I had been smarter at figuring this whole thing out earlier on in my life, BUT we all know the what-if game never helped anyone.

I continued on with my counseling throughout the summer and fall months, and during that time I confidently walked right back into the church that I had so quickly abandoned five months earlier. This time, the real, transparent Amy showed up, and that's who they got this time. No more putting on a front, but the real, raw, broken warrior-in-the-making was very present for once. God sent along so many mentors in my life with whom I was able to be real and transparent. I finally had accountability in my life, and what a breath of fresh air that was for me. It was hard those first few months of healing. I know I called and texted my mentors with every emotional meltdown I was fighting. I was still learning coping skills. I saw through two of these women's stories that my marriage with Will could be restored, and I knew that was what God was calling me to do.

I'm not going to lie – our relationship has had its rocky moments. Will still had a lot of healing of his own to do, and I could not help him with that (other than praying and living out what God had done and was continually doing in me). I threw myself into every Bible study and opportunity to grow spiritually that I could. I was on a mission to root out everything in me that wasn't of God, becoming the warrior that God had called me to be (and that Satan was scared I would become!). I learned and starting applying my spiritual armor just like it says in the book of Ephesians. I prayed and I studied, and I grew deeper and deeper. I found that I was not having my emotional breakdowns in Bible study class anymore. The things that once caused me so much fear now were fuel to push me forward. I began to share my story, piece by piece, and as I told what had happened and what God had done, I became stronger and stronger. The very things that Satan tried to use to destroy me became the very things that God was using as mortar under each brick He was placing.

On October 1st, the Carrie Underwood song, "There Must Be Something In The Water" became very personal to me. Yes, I know the "water" doesn't have any power in it, BUT the act itself was something right out of heaven. I was rebaptized and rededicated my life to God. When my pastor pushed me under the water, something powerful started happening, like the Spirit of God washing over me. When I came up, it seemed to be in slow motion. Yes, I had been saved as a child, but thank God for His Grace. Nothing I did or ever could do could take that away!

I was His.

Even though growing up I worried I wasn't saved all the time, and I mean ALL the time, I tried to be perfect, stressed out over being saved "enough." I couldn't get it through my head that it was just that easy. It was as if I had to be as perfect as I could. I bet I prayed for Jesus to come into my heart every week, and on some days multiple times. Every church revival I prayed the prayer. I wrestled with the panic that I didn't say it right or do it right. I struggled with this, well until my BIG oops in life. It's crazy how with all the imperfections from then on that I would be the most confident in my salvation, but not in my purpose.

In January, it was every evident what God had been doing those past seven months. But God had one last thing He had to show me, and He did it through another Bible study. The name of the Bible study was "Burdens to Blessings: Discover The Power Of Your Story." It was the first session, and I was pumped. *"Let's get this thing moving"*, I thought. Our teacher had invited a special guest to present this study and do a kickoff. She told us all about the woman who wrote the study, and I immediately fell in love with what I was hearing. My thoughts were, *"This is exactly what I've been doing, facing my burdens head on."* Oh, I was excited! The lady told us about seminars that the author of the study, Kim Crabill put on, and she said one was coming up in a few weeks in Georgia. My stomach had butterflies; I could not even wait! I grabbed my phone and began to search, to find out about Kim Crabill. I found her on Facebook, and oh, my gosh! She accepted my friend request! Really! This "very important person" just accepted me! No way! As I looked more and more into this seminar, I knew I was supposed to go. I began to read her book the following day.

As I planned my trip to Georgia, I prayed for a sign that I should go. I continued reading in the first chapter of Kim Crabill's book that we are challenged to face our burdens. I thought of how I had been doing this very same thing for the past few months, and I knew it worked. Something inside of me told me to ask God to show me anything that I might not have faced yet, although again I was sure I had faced it all. My prayer was over, but before the day was ended, God showed me through something my daughter said, "Yes Amy, there is something else."

In that very moment as I sat on my daughter's bed listening to her talk about how hard it is to live in two houses, I knew I had to face this very painful, ugly thing that had destroyed me for so long. It was the BIG IT (my first divorce) that I was too afraid and weak to face. Before, it would have ended with me having an emotional breakdown that would leave me curled up in the fetal position for who knows how long. *"God, if I could choose, I really do not want to go there. Is there any other way around this? God, I have already been working hard and faced so many other things. Is that not enough?"* God said, "Amy, this is where it all began. This, out of all the burdens, is the most painful."

I wrestled with this and said, "Alright God, I'll go there if You promise You will be there with me through each moment and each thought." One by one, I faced each choice I had made before that divorce; it was like walking into a room. The room was full of words, flashes of faces, actions and things of which I was so ashamed. There was heartache in the rooms constructed out of my choices and actions that led to that first divorce. *Oh no, there that one is, please God, please be with me; it hurts so bad, BUT lets do this! I am strong enough now through You!* As each memory played out with all the pain, I asked God to heal it once and for all. Before that, though, I really had to confront it and see it for what it was and open myself up to the raw pain so that real healing could take place. This went on throughout the night, but I was determined not to stop until I had faced it all. It played out from beginning to end just like a movie; as I sat and watched, tears covered my face at times and I felt gut-wrenching pain that hurt so deeply. That is why I had not face it before; it was too painful. I made sure not to skip anything because I wanted God's healing touch on everything that was broken in me.

One week later I flew out to Georgia to the Kim Crabill seminar and still was in the process of going through all these things. God had finishing touches waiting for me there at that seminar. During the seminar, a brown bag with tissue paper sat in front of each person at each table. At the end of the seminar, Kim asked us to look inside the brown bag; what awaited me in the bag of my dirty, ugly mess was a beautiful crown. Kim said, "Ladies, this whole time your crown has been waiting right there in what you were so scared to face." She asked all of us to make a circle, and she came to each woman and placed their crown on their heads. I completely lost it when she stood in front of me and placed my crown on my head. It was the final ending to my long, drawn-out story. I was and always had been the Daughter of a King!

As I looked in the mirror at my one-dollar crown, I felt like I was the wealthiest person in the world. I said, "NOTHING can take this from me and nothing ever will again! I am royalty. I am a princess. I thought of all the time, money and energy I had spent chasing after that Mrs. Texas crown for four years and how in order to get it I had to change everything about myself from my hair to the way I spoke. But that earthly crown was only attainable with perfection and doing something that the Bible tells me not to do.

**"Do not conform to the pattern of this world but be transformed by the renewing of your mind. Then you will be able to test and approve what God's will is – his good, pleasing and perfect will." - Romans 12:22**

I came home ready to share my story, ALL of it. I knew that by being transparent and vulnerable others would see that they, too, could face the very things that kept them in darkness for far too long. I had a passion burning inside to tell everyone what God can do with their ugly stuff, the ugly parts that they hope no one ever finds out about and those they try to forget themselves. I began sharing my life day by day and opened up with complete transparency about who I was and what I had done and what God had done. God had brought me through it all and surprisingly in one piece. He poured into me His strength so that I could stand strong and speak, with my head held high, about the very things that tried to destroy my life.

One year after Will and I had divorced, we stood with our children, our mentors and my family to remarry. We were going to remarry on our anniversary, January 28, but I did not want to because I was not doing anything without our children there to witness this new covenant. One week after what would have been our seventh anniversary, Will and I became husband and wife again. BUT this time, I had a smile on my face and confidence in my God living in me. I committed to be the wife God called me to be and to be an example of Christ's commitment. Through Will, God showed me what grace looked like in human form. Will gave me grace when it was undeserved and took on the debt I had (result of my sin) as his own. Now what picture is painted from that? YES!! Jesus!

**"But God demonstrates his own love for us in this: While we were sinners, Christ died for us." - Romans 5:8**

So to you ladies that are headed to the well, head hung in shame, weary and worn, praying you do not run into anyone who may know you—you don't want anyone to know about the hurt, pain and shame that you carry in secret. You have anxiety just thinking about the very fact that someone might know about that "thing." You think, *"Will anyone understand how or why I've gotten to where I am and have done the things I've done?"* Well, I'm your gal! I completely understand and I can point out every rock I've crawled under and every hole I ran into because of that same fear. As you're headed throughout your day, Jesus is patiently waiting for you to believe what He says about you and not the lies the enemy has led you to believe all this time.

Take that scary first step of faith, turn to God and

ask for help. With that, ask Him to help you face the very things that hurt you so badly, the things that pick at you and haunt you day in and day out. We believe the lie that it's all better left in the dark – I mean, we have all heard the saying, "Don't air out your dirty laundry." I tell you, air it all out to someone you trust! Run out into your yard and let it out! Piece by piece, air it out so that true healing can begin. I'm living proof that someone can be too far gone in the world's eyes for anything good to become of their life. But NOT in the eyes of God's.

Listen, I know what embarrassment from "wrong choices" looks like, especially when it comes to the world's view of me – I mean, I'm sure I am banned from changing my name EVER AGAIN at the DMV. It still stings a little  when my credit report is pulled and I'm asked, "Ma'am, which last name do you prefer?" Yep, it's a mess. My past and the pain with it is not pretty. Now, instead of drowning in shame from those names, my focus is on what Christ is doing through those many last "names."

There will always be "those" who look down at me as they laugh saying, "You change your name more than I change my handbags." Yep, there will always be those with their opinions. That's the amazing part of facing those dirty things head on. Once you have made peace with them you can walk in confidence of Whose you are! To those with their opinions, you can respond with, "I know! That was me then, but isn't God amazing?" No matter what you're probably saying right now, "Well, Amy, you just don't know what I've done." Let me say this, maybe not. BUT I know what Jesus did and IT IS FINISHED! DO you hear that?

DONE. OVER. Nothing else owed.

The very things I held my head low over are the very things that God has used for His purpose, and He has created beautiful opportunities in my life to share who HE is, not who I am. You have just read about Amy when she's in control. As I write my last few sentences, know that I have written this book with YOU in mind. The girl in the closet. The broken one. Ashamed and carrying all the guilt in every way and every day of your life. I SEE you, and you are so much more than that which you carry.

This is not just the testimony I never wanted; it's our testimony. The little girl we once were never wanted all of this. Now, with the testimony that is ours, let's allow that little girl inside us to know that she can be okay, and in spite of the brokenness she made it! And just like my friend Stephanie told me once, "Rise sister, and if you don't know what to say, just say Jesus. There is Power in the Name of Jesus!"

# ABOUT THE AUTHOR

Amy was raised on her parents' dairy farm just outside of Rusk, Texas in the Atoy Community where she learned the importance of hard work and the blessing of working as a family. From raising baby calves, to long, hot summer days on a tractor in the hay field, Amy loved her life and always tried to find the good in every situation. It wasn't until Amy experienced her own personal failings that she found it hard to see the good in her own life.

After her introduction to that ugly thing called shame, Amy struggled for years with feelings of worthlessness, believing that nothing good could come of her life because of her past mistakes. These thoughts only led to more poor choices that ended in losing everything. Finally able to see everything more clearly, she found that all God's promises in His Word were true. She finally believed God and His promise – He took the dirtiest of things and created the most beautiful, even in her life.

Amy Blackwell lives in a small East Texas town with her husband, Will, their four children, and a few goats. She has committed her life to sharing her real, raw and relatable story with those that are where she once was. She battles through her own shortcomings to speak out. She knows very well where you might be right now; experiencing the shame that has paralyzed you from moving forward. "It's hard for me to speak in public, and I struggle with extreme social anxiety at times," shares Amy. "I also have a problem of chasing those pesky squirrels that live in my mind when speaking, but I fight through all my weakness for that one lady who is feeling worthless and alone. I know she is worth the fight."

# ACKNOWLEDGMENT

To my Momma and Daddy: Paula and the late Steve Helm, thank you for teaching me about Jesus as a child, so that I could find my way back to Him as an adult. I am thankful to God for the blessing of being your daughter and have the honor of carrying on your legacy.

To my herd: Will and the kids, the love and passion I have for you all pushes me to fight each day to be the best godly wife and Momma I can be.

My villagers: Melissa and Stephanie, you both are my devil fighting, spiritual guiding and godly influencers. You both have been a source of support and wisdom in my weakness as in my strengths. Oh, and I can't forget all those late-night armor repair visits.

Kim Crabill, my mentor and friend: Thank you for your obedience to God and sharing your story so that I could see the importance in sharing mine. Just as your mom did for you, you gave me the best gift, and it will keep moving down throughout the generations to come.

My city on a hill: I would like to thank all the ones who have encouraged me throughout my healing and my writing journey. You know who you are. There is no way I could've reach this without God placing each one of you along my path, some who were complete stranglers that have become some of my dearest friends. I am extremely blessed by you, and you are very much loved by me.

My crown, Stephanie Goode: Thank you for your

obedience to God. It was in that, you were used on a day that you probably thought was just another ordinary one, but that day forever changed my life. You made yourself ready and willing to be used, and God poured into you what He needed me to know about myself--not judgment but love and with an anointed plan of the direction He wanted me to go.

CPSIA information can be obtained
at www.ICGtesting.com
Printed in the USA
LVHW080552150821
695353LV00012B/681

9 780578 607009